SELL

For dear Frank

with great admiration

warm regards

Subroto

SUBROTO BAGCHI

SELL

THE ART, THE SCIENCE, THE WITCHCRAFT

 hachette
INDIA

First published in 2017 by Hachette India
(Registered name: Hachette Book Publishing India Pvt. Ltd)
An Hachette UK company
www.hachetteindia.com

1

ISBN 978-93-5009-582-9

Hachette Book Publishing India Pvt. Ltd
4th & 5th Floors, Corporate Centre,
Plot No. 94, Sector 44, Gurugram – 122003, India

Typeset in Guardi Lt Std 10/16.8
by Inosoft Systems, Noida

Printed and bound in India
by Manipal Technologies Limited, Manipal

To Sonoma

CONTENTS

CONTENTS / viii

INTRODUCTION

I N THE LAST FORTY years of my working life, I have played several roles in the world of business. Having begun as a lower-division clerk in a government office, I eventually became the executive chairman of Mindtree, one of India's most admired software services companies, the first venture capital-funded IT services company in the country to go all the way from an idea to an initial public offering (IPO). By the end of 2016, Mindtree (established in 1999) employed 16,000 people in locations across the globe and was featured in *Fortune* magazine's Top 500 Most Valuable Companies list. In May 2016, at the invitation of the Government of Odisha,

I took on the full-time, pro-bono role of Chairman of the newly created Odisha Skill Development Authority. Standing where I am today, the tags that I wear may read 'entrepreneur', 'business-leader', 'author' and 'public servant', among others. But, even when taken together, these convey very little about the *skills* I possess.

Some may be surprised to read this, but possibly the most defining skill I have learnt and practised in my life has been that of salesmanship. Of the thirty years I have spent getting up every morning to go to work, I was a salesman on the road for more than ten. In my professional life, I have been an entrepreneur on two occasions: First with Project.21, my first venture in the IT services sector, and then with Mindtree. When I look back I find that it was as an entrepreneur that my selling skills, honed in earlier jobs, proved to be the most valuable. Whether I was closing a new customer acquisition, getting a better deal on a bank loan, negotiating a smarter lease while renting space or convincing a potential employee to sign on the dotted line – I was performing the core actions of a salesperson. Now, with the Odisha Skill Development Authority, my responsibility is to skill about eight lakh young men and women, mostly school dropouts. In that capacity, I have to sell concepts, ideas and action every day to a large eco-system of stakeholders – from government agencies and private skill-development partners to the young men and women themselves as well as their parents so that they opt for skill-training over general education, as well as the potential employers who will hire them as trainees.

Today, if you are a professional in a role that requires you to get people to buy into your idea (or your product, or your vision), you have to know how to sell. Think of the president or the prime minister of a nation; the chief executive of a profit – or, in equal measure, a non-profit–organization; an account director at an advertising agency; a partner at a traditional consultancy or a law firm; the medical director of a super-speciality hospital; a fund manager of an investment firm; the country head of an aid organization; or an account manager at a bank cross-selling products to high net-worth clients – all of them have to ensure they are heard, that they forge a consensus, gather commitment and deliver an end goal. In short, they are all intimately engaged in the act of *selling*.

Very few professionals, including those mentioned above, however, consider this aspect – salesmanship – to be critical to their careers, and rarely give this skill the attention it deserves. In fact, not only do people not recognize the pervasiveness of selling as an act, but some are also wary of it. Take, for instance, this interesting incident: I happen to be among the board of directors of a large enterprise. In one of the board briefings, an executive was presenting his views on the success of a credit card they had co-branded with a financial institution. While speaking of the features that had worked for them, he suddenly stopped in his tracks and qualified, 'Please don't think I am selling the card to you.'

I immediately rose to my feet and asked, 'But why not?'

The truth is, even among the most knowledgeable professionals, selling is seen as an act of invasion, something that denotes vested, even veiled, interest. Yet, when you think about it, every time we face a job interview, or argue a case for additional funding for a given project, or tackle any similar situation, we risk losing the deal of the day without the ability to sell.

Just as the act of selling is seen in a restricted light, many people have a very staid image of a salesperson. This book has been written to encourage you to take a wider view and bring you face-to-face with sales professionals who are nothing close to staid. They are quintessential salespeople – they have knowledge, they have intuition, they have wisdom, they have sagacity, they have empathy, they possess the power of persuasion, they have the energy to persist and the will to see their commitment through. They exhibit skills that sometimes border on pure wizardry. Their stories and their wisdom will open up to you an altogether different perspective of selling as a skill. For selling is no longer a profession in itself. It is a key component for professional success in *every* field, an essential skill for people at all levels in any organization to possess.

I am not a great fan of spelling out what you should take away from this book and I am not saying you need to put your learnings into practice from tomorrow to see the benefits knock on your door. Life doesn't quite work that way. Most long-term lessons of life and conduct take place in our mind, in a space of silence and non-knowledge. But this I can tell you – whatever you take away from this book will make you more impactful in your organizational role, more effective in persuasive communication – no matter what the situation may be – and more confident in every way.

■

THE
ESSENTIALS

Selling is not something to be apologetic about.

It is not about hustling.

It is not about conmanship.

It is not about being invasive or intrusive.

It is definitive persuasion with a clear end goal.

Irrespective of what people are selling and what type of doors they may be knocking at, the basics of selling remain the same.

There is a process, a rhythm and a certain nuance to it – and it goes thus:

Look at me.

Listen to me.

Buy my words

even before you buy my wares.

Let's agree on the terms of our transaction.

Now tell everyone about me.

And come back for more.

How artfully this message is conveyed and how efficiently it is executed determines the chances of success.

Selling is *not* a pushy, winner-take-all, masculine act.

It is an empathy-led, process-driven and knowledge-intensive discipline.

Because, in the end, people buy from people.

THE
THREE-LEGGED
STOOL

A STOOL SITS PERFECTLY only when its three legs are of the exact same length and shape. But wait! The three legs also have to be equally strong. Selling can be described as a three-legged stool: part art, part science and part witchcraft, all in equal measure.

Selling Is One-third Art

My wife, Susmita, and I were in a mall for the express purpose of buying a pair of trousers for me. I have always resisted buying clothes, which gets Susmita hassled because she has taken it upon herself to ensure that I am always appropriately attired. As for me, I believe I have an overstocked wardrobe and, in any case, find shopping for clothes not the best use of my time. But I would, of course, cancel a meeting to gawk at a newly released racing bike by a specialist vehicle manufacturer or a new DSLR camera by Nikon.

Susmita knows my weaknesses well.

'If you come along,' she had said to me on this occasion, 'I will let you buy the 500-mm Sigma lens you wanted. It is on sale online, I noticed.' I am a sucker for camera accessories. I buy new ones all the time though they mostly remain unused since I am more attached to the ones I already possess. Susmita is usually given to thwarting my attempts to buy more camera-related equipment but, knowing my soft spot, she had gone straight for the throat this time around. I knew she was offering me a deal: Buy one, get one... Well, not free, perhaps, but the offer was irresistible.

I was prepared, however, and once we were in the clothing store, I stealthily laid bare my secret weapon. After trying out the first pair of trousers in the men's section, I complained that the design – clearly in vogue – was fitted below the navel, tight at the waist and narrow at the bottom. It just wasn't who I was, I declared.

'Just look,' I said, indicating my trusted comfort-wear, 'at my khakis.'

The young sales lady attending to us had stood by silently till then. Now she spoke up gently. 'Those pants you're wearing, sir,' she said apologetically, 'went out of fashion thirty years ago.'

I looked down at my pants, admittedly through fresh eyes. *She appears to have called me Rip Van Winkle*, I mused. I wanted to take offence; I wanted to think she was being rude. But when I looked up at her she smiled disarmingly and, holding out a fresh pair, said, 'Here is something that is both contemporary and comfortable. Sir, give this one a try.'

I turned to Susmita. 'Okay,' I said, 'let me try out the one she is suggesting.'

Inside the trial room, the young lady's voice kept echoing in my ears: 'out of fashion, out of fashion, out of fashion'. It became clear to me that I was holding on to my khaki trousers as the only possible bridge to my fading youth. I came out of the trial room and told Susmita in a voice of feigned nonchalance, 'It's okay, I guess.' To which she firmly said, 'Now that we're here, I might as well pick up the other shades of these trousers. Who knows when you will have the time to shop again.'

The incident reminded me of another time, many years ago, when Susmita had dragged me to a store to buy me new shoes. My mind is hazy about what she had offered me as inducement at the time, but I had been far more docile back then. I remember trying out a new pair of black shoes.

As soon as I'd said, 'Fine, I will take this pair,' Susmita had moved in deftly.

'Now that you like the feel, and the price is good,

you should get a pair of brown ones. You really need them.'

'No,' I said firmly. 'Look at the shoes I'm wearing. They're so good.'

The shoe salesman, who had so far been letting Susmita do his job, chipped in. 'Sir, those shoes you're wearing have already become members of the million-mile club!'

Susmita had won. The salesman had won. And both of them knew it.

A successful salesperson takes selling to the level of an art. They figure out quickly who the buyer is and what they must say to them, as well as when and how they must say it. They are good at languages and at reading emotions and know how to choose their moment perfectly. They are experts at their work. The lady selling me the trousers had got away with a statement about what went out of fashion thirty years ago even though she probably hadn't been born then. She could do that not because she was expertise-led but because, like the shoe salesman, she was confident of the moment and the metaphor.

Selling Is One-third Science

In the last three decades, we have learnt more about how the brain works than in the history of humanity. This has largely been made possible because three disciplines have come together: Neuroscience, imaging and psychology. Thanks to imaging, we can actually see how parts of the brain react to any stimulation. Neuroscience is able to show us the relationship between brain cells and the process of thought itself. Psychology is more accurately able to explain why we behave the way we do.

The process of buying and selling happens in the brain. Depending on how we sell, different chemicals are released in the brain that can trigger a wide variety of responses, like fear, anxiety, joy, comfort and trust. As a result of our fresh scientific understanding of the brain and human behaviour, new studies have been launched under such labels as 'the neuroscience of selling'. This is not just about how and why we buy from one salesperson and not the other. It extends to machine learning because, thanks to online shopping, we are constantly buying from machines.

When you're browsing through Amazon's website and a message appears telling you that people who bought what you just did also bought this or that or the other, you have just been spoken to directly by science. The message being communicated to you is the work of an intelligent algorithm probably created by half-a-dozen PhDs in subjects like pure mathematics, computer science, neuroscience and psychology. This algorithm can zip through petabytes of data in the flash of an eye – what we call *big data* – to deliver what is called *personalization*. It is the holy grail of the digital world. You, the buyer, love it because your 'personal page' is telling you you are special, right from welcoming you in to reminding you what you have purchased or browsed for before, recommending products in sync with your searches and keeping you updated on offers and discounts that will enable you to make a fully informed choice. So you browse and pause and add something to the shopping cart that wasn't on your to-buy list just minutes, even seconds, ago.

There are many things you like to check out online but prefer to buy in a store after you've had a chance to touch and feel the product and talk to a human being. So you step into the store on a Sunday morning for a large-screen LCD television, a washing machine or noise-cancelling cordless headphones. But, unlike the World Wide Web, the brick-and-mortar store does not recognize you. The store does not say, 'Welcome back.' The salesperson who walks up to you as soon as you have spent five seconds ogling at the floor model of the television doesn't really know what you bought the last time, what you returned, what your lifetime purchase has been and your credit preference while financing a high-value purchase. Imagine, if in real time, the salesperson had the benefit of the science that your personalized homepage has?

Today, we are getting to where we want to be faster than anticipated with the help of technology. What was earlier based solely on intuition and close observation, and the intelligent application of both, has now been given new impetus by technology. Intuition can now be backed and reinforced by data and fact, and data itself can be mined endlessly, not only to refine the knowledge of buying patterns and consumer behaviour but also to predict future patterns and trends, and reduce risks to business initiatives. Much of it is ready. Some of it has still to contend with issues of privacy and ethics and regulation. But a lot – a whole lot – is quickly moving from the virtual to the real world.

Consider this: Today, I expect my banker to know my account details and credit score and even my spending habits before even speaking to me. I expect a newly joined sales representative to know not just my current purchase but the history of my customer relationship. That is why Customer Relationship Management (CRM) tools today have become indispensable for salespeople. Thanks to the constantly improving quality of machine intelligence, which figures out who I may be as a buyer and how to sell to me, our expectations from actual people entrusted with the job of selling to us is vastly changing. Gone are the days of carrying pamphlets in a briefcase; organizing sales apps on the smart phone have now elevated sales to the realm of science.

Selling Is One-third Witchcraft

While selling is an art and is today increasingly driven by science and technology, it also resides in the exalted realm of witchcraft. A lot of selling is about magic.

Go to any organization and you will hear of people who are or have been legends when it comes to selling a product, a service or an idea. Their ability goes beyond mastering the art and the science; they have near-magical powers to create something out of nothing. Send them to a hopeless land where no one before them has ever found anything and they return with deals. Send them to a rigid, obstinate, permanent hater of what you provide and they come back with a smile and a signed cheque.

The old adage goes: He can sell ice cream to Eskimos and coal to Newcastle. To be able to pull off that feat, these people possess special qualities that make them Druid-like. Druids, if you remember, were learned men of wisdom, revered as philosophers and teachers in the ancient world. At times they functioned as priests and soothsayers, and were also known for their acts of magic or sorcery that had roots in their vast knowledge of the physical and natural world.

In sales terms, the phenomenal ability to sell is a combination of vast knowledge of the art and the science of selling processes, intuition and personal character traits, which help cast a spell (in a good way, of course) through powers of persuasion and the story that is created around organizations and ideas, products and services. How a narrative is put together, how engagingly it is delivered, how it is used to build anticipation and eagerness to move on to the next process of the act is what I term as 'witchcraft'.

How do these 'Druids' do it, you might ask. Can anyone ever be like them?

In my career, I have seen many such Druids at work. This book is, in fact, replete with encounters with wizards among salespeople whom I sought out for the express purpose of getting their wisdom across to you. There is much to learn from them through keen observation and apprenticeship.

So, get ready to sit on the three-legged stool; observe and listen, and apply these lessons to your daily work life.

■

PANNING FOR GOLD

Information on prospective buyers may come from the most unlikely sources. It is only through diligent and uninhibited prospecting that you will uncover game-changing deals.

MY FIRST SALES JOB, back in 1981, was that of a computer salesman. That is how I came into the Information Technology (IT) industry. I am indebted to this part of my career, because this is where I learned a considerable amount about the art, science and witchcraft of selling.

My sales territory at the time consisted of Rajasthan, Madhya Pradesh and parts of Delhi, where I sold computers to first-time computer buyers. Each computer – at the time a machine less powerful than the dumbest of today's smartphones, equipped with two floppy-disk drives and 64 kilobytes of RAM, along with a small printer – was worth ₹4,00,000, a sizeable fortune. My target buyers were owners of medium-scale businesses: The businessmen and women who ran trading houses and small factories, owned rice mills or operated mines. Often, the firms that I did business with had begun as small, family-run enterprises a generation or two ago and then prospered and grown into mid-size businesses. The new-generation owners of such firms could afford air conditioners in their offices, usually owned more than one car and aspired to work with gadgets beyond their desk calculators.

In 1981, there were predominantly two kinds of computer companies that dominated the Indian market. There were the multinationals who sold mainframe machines and did job work for corporations through their data centres, and there were a few well-established Indian business houses offering mini-computers based on later technology. The buyers of mainframes and mini-computers were large companies with very sophisticated clientele.

It was around this time that microprocessor-based desktop computers arrived for the first time in India. These were relatively less expensive than their predecessors and spurred a few start-up companies. Mine was one such. But, as a start-up in those early days of start-ups and computer technology, we did not yet have the pedigree to get past the gates of the big buyers of the day. It was largely because of this reason that our company tried something innovative. Rather than seek legitimacy in a market in which we would have a hard time finding acceptance, our company decided to open up to the hitherto unknown first-time user segment – small- and medium-scale businesses with no prior experience in using computers.

Mostly the offices of the clients we pursued were not located in plush areas like Connaught Circus, Bhikaji Kama or Nehru Place, as the major corporates were. Often they did not have 'corporate offices' at all, and their owners or managers occupied office space within their factories, usually located in places like Naraina, Ghaziabad and Faridabad, and their small-town counterparts. For me, as I hit the streets on my Yezdi motorbike, the first step in finding prospective clients was to locate window air conditioners and multiple cars in the driveway – sure signs at the time of the office premises of businesspeople in need of the product I was peddling. I had planned out my routine pretty well around these basics.

A lot of my search for my particular segment of buyers took me to small cities and large towns in neighbouring states. The standard routine was an overnight bus or train ride, checking into a hotel on arrival, getting ready, hiring an auto-rickshaw for the day and setting off in search of offices that flaunted the familiar markers – a smart signboard, perhaps, window air conditioners and at least two cars in the driveway. In an unknown town, though, I always made it a point to be armed beforehand with information. I treated the town or city as a new landmass at which I had arrived with the aim of discovering a peoples or even gold. If I could catch the pulse of the place and its culture, and map the relevant information in my head, my job, I knew, would become much easier and the cold calls I made would have more chances of a successful outcome.

My first task was thus to seek out the manager of the hotel I was staying at – always a formidable source of information and, by virtue of his profession, approachable and helpful. Usually the hotel managers turned out to be veritable encyclopaedias: I would enquire after the major businessmen in the area, the factories and businesses that were doing well, the ones that were seeing bad days or closing down, the areas where the more prosperous people lived, and even where they ate and entertained themselves. After the hotel manager, I would turn my attention to locating the local chartered accountants. People in this line of business know many things. For instance, they would know the pain points of their customers or which of their clients had enough money and was progressive enough to buy and install a computer. But, unlike the hotel managers, they tended to be reclusive. By building trust and confidence, and presenting something useful to tell or show them, I often won their confidence and managed to get hold of the valuable information I was after.

There were other people, like the head of the local computer installation centre at a central government laboratory, or the principal of the local engineering college, or the head of the local industry association, who served as starting points of my search for lucrative business. Conversations with these people almost invariably led me to draw up a reliable list of prospective buyers I could approach.

While this technique worked very well in small places, Delhi proved to be a more difficult market to crack. In the capital city, everyone had an office, an air conditioner and at least two cars. The helpful guides that I had identified for small towns would be of no help here. While the rest of the sales team, of which I was a part, were breaking their heads over it, an ingenious manager in the firm hit upon a golden idea to crack open the Delhi market. He was able to obtain a list of the people in the city who paid sales tax to the government. Leaving aside the legality of possessing this information, the team now had a ready list of business-owners in the city to follow up on. The difficulty was that this list did not reveal the exact size of the businesses. To use sales terminology, this list didn't have 'prospects', it had 'suspects' – that is, the larger pool of people from among whom prospects emerge – and needed on-the-ground research and qualification. Each of us sales executives were handed a list based on the assigned territory. Armed with this list and my trusty steed (yes, the

Yezdi), I made sure I spent half of my day, every day that I was covering Delhi, looking for opportunities. It was a lot of work, sometimes leading to very unexpected outcomes – some successful, some painful and some downright surreal.

Consider, for instance, the day when, guided by my unreferenced but vast list of 'suspects', I descended upon New Delhi's G.B. Road area. G.B. Road was then, as it is today, earmarked by its flourishing brothels, an unlikely place to find someone who would buy a computer. But selling as a profession thrives on nothing if not the fuel of optimism. You wake up on the bleakest of mornings and tell yourself: *Let's go for it, because, who knows! After all, if you don't try you won't know what's out there.* So there I was on G.B. Road, looking for the usual signs – windows with air conditioners. For all I knew, there could be a progressive Lalaji (a term of respect for local businessmen) in the area; perhaps an owner of six rice mills in Punjab, living a frugal life; or a businessman running his multi-crore business from an understated address. Or, maybe, someone who had arrived in Delhi as a refugee from Lahore and settled in the G.B. Road area because, well, the rent was low, and was now the owner of a flourishing trade.

My optimism took me deep into the lanes of the area, and the deeper I went the emptier the streets looked to me. Not losing hope, however, I treaded on. At length I spotted a group of women at the far end of the lane, almost at the same time as they spotted me. The next moment, much to my surprise, some of the ladies began running toward me, uttering shrill, angry cries and displaying every suggestion of hostility in their charge. It took me a moment to realize what had happened. The ladies had been in the middle of conducting some kind of a puja or ritual in which outsiders were not meant to intrude. Not knowing that I was an innocent computer salesman wandering their streets misled by data and optimism, they had presumed that my untimely arrival was for a completely different purpose. In any case, this was not a moment for reflection. I turned my bike around, wedged my briefcase as securely as I could between my stomach and the lid of the gas tank, and made the quickest getaway of my life.

Every successful salesperson has his repertoire of interesting stories, of unanticipated success, near misses and anti-climactic episodes in the prospecting process. While prospecting, you will sometimes end up working for days without seeing a lead, let alone one that can be qualified. Yet, it is only through diligent and uninhibited prospecting that you will uncover game-changing deals. And this does not apply to pure-play salespeople alone. At times, non-sales professionals involved in solutioning at various levels in their organizations are required to smell out opportunities, engage with clients even before a need is felt, and ferret out opportunities and subsequent business.

The idea that prospecting is successful only when a particular connection and negotiation results in a closed deal is a narrow way of viewing the sales process. Many connections that you make when you are out prospecting may yield rewards of different kinds. They could, for instance, lead to completely new, unanticipated possibilities.

A few years after my G.B. Road misadventure, I was chasing an opportunity at the Railway Design and Standardization Organization (RDSO) in Lucknow. This is the research and development (R&D) arm of the Indian Railways. I used to visit the RDSO offices as part of a computer deal with the electrical engineering department. We had installed a computer there and things weren't going well. The joint director in charge – a serious man and a fine scientist – however, didn't let that come in the way of how he felt about me. One day, while I was there, I asked him to explain the structure of the RDSO as a whole, including the departments beyond his purview. This, too, was prospecting on my part; large organizations have similar complexities, challenges and opportunities that towns or cities possess, and the rules of prospecting apply equally to both. The gentleman obliged and, on a late Saturday afternoon, as he sat patiently answering my queries and drawing for me the entire map of the organization, he paused and told me that I should perhaps be meeting his counterpart in the mechanical engineering department.

The following week, I met another scientist and though there was no deal on the table, I discovered through our conversation that he was excited about the possibility of computerizing the maintenance process of locomotive engines. This was going to be big for the Railways because they were phasing out steam engines. It was also going to be an elaborate project as the solution being provided needed to be proved via a pilot project. I jumped in, and once I was given access to a locomotive maintenance yard I learnt how loco-engines were maintained over the next couple of months. Based on the study, I put together a solution framework and a prototype that the RDSO thought was good enough to be presented at an annual conference of the heads of all locomotive maintenance sheds in the country.

I was beside myself presenting to a group like that. I had been a student of humanities, and here I was, all of twenty-five, telling an audience of experts and scientists how they could automate something as complex as the periodic maintenance of a locomotive. Eventually, we won the contract to deploy the solution at the locomotive shed where we had done the study. But, more importantly, it was a turning point in my career. It was my first experience of finding an opportunity, conducting a study, working with others within my company and putting together and then selling a complete, packaged solution to a client. It was at this point that – without knowing the term at the time – I moved from selling to 'solutioning'. This single project brought me a long way and I have always believed that it all began with the eagerness with which I was prospecting at the RDSO.

A little less than a decade later, I found myself in Silicon Valley, where my job was to establish a beachhead for Wipro. I was charged with enticing tech companies in the Valley to award contract R&D assignments to Wipro's research wing. This was at a time when most executives in American companies did not know where India was.

After landing in the Valley, I began prospecting by mapping organizations of all kinds that had an India connection and, through their members, finding those individuals who could lead to opportunities. One such was the Silicon Valley Indian Professionals Association (SIPA) that periodically held meetings for its members and invited outsiders to speak. I managed to get invited to one of their meetings, where I met a gentleman who had come to attend it out of curiosity. We exchanged business cards customarily and went our own ways. But within the next few months, he took up a very important position at a large company in the Valley and called me to discuss an opportunity. It led to a massive multi-year deal – a big business basket for Wipro. When I look back, that win is one of the major factors that eventually shaped my destiny in later years because of the experience and visibility it gave me.

Many salespeople settle down in their careers and gradually lose the ability to prospect. The idea of prospecting is to look for and open the keys to new territories, be it a new area or a new account. It leads you to try and sell your product to someone you have sought out, whom you didn't know before and who doesn't necessarily have a stated need for what you are selling. Many salespeople prefer to have qualified, ready leads fed to them by their organizations so that they can simply convert the ready prospect into a customer. But the best salespeople never give up prospecting and cold calling because the process keeps their spirit of inquiry alive; they know that every bit of knowledge they glean from the process will add to them as people and professionals.

Being an ace prospector requires overcoming hesitation and awkwardness, being bold and intrepid and not taking rejection to heart. Successful prospecting begins with a genuine interest and curiosity in people and places, particular processes and larger happenings in the world at large. Then, of course, other things follow.

But first you must seek. As you seek and you discover, you begin to feel the wonder of a Hiuen Tsang, a Christopher

Columbus or a Charles Darwin. They weren't just explorers focused on discovering something phenomenal at the end of their quest; they enjoyed every bit of the process that reaching the end entailed.

■

FISHING IN THE RIGHT POND

The key to good prospecting is proper segmentation and qualification of 'suspects'. The basic question to apply your mind to is: What is in the deal for the buyer?

A CLOSE FRIEND WHO is the chairman of a very active not-for-profit organization (more commonly called non-governmental organizations or NGOs) called me one day. Profit or not-for-profit, every organization needs money. In the case of the latter, someone has to buy into what you stand for in terms of the cause you espouse, and that someone must also be sure about what is in it for him in order to part with his money so that you can pay your bills.

My friend wanted to discuss fundraising with me. His organization was running into problems while working on long-acting projects that needed multiple-year commitments from donors – a mix of high net-worth individuals, public- and private-sector companies who had funds for corporate social responsibility and charities that, in turn, funded charities.

The reality is that India has now spawned more than 3.1 million NGOs that seek to solve social problems – a number that could perhaps be more than the quantum of social problems out there. All these NGOs approach the same sources for money and flood them with requests for sponsorship. Thus, for the first time, the organization my friend had co-founded many years ago found itself having to pitch for funds. From what he described, it wasn't going well, and that was due to two reasons: First, there was severe competition out there from other NGOs and, second, his own organization seemed to lack the ability to sell their purpose and attract funds. Not that they were incompetent or that they did not try hard enough – they were good people, driven by their altruistic agenda – but they were simply not able to get sponsors on board. The continuous negative outcome of their sales efforts was making the team frustrated, affecting their morale and causing them to let go of the easiest chances of raising funds.

I agreed to spend a Saturday with his team trying to get to the root of the problem, to see if I could perhaps nudge them in the right direction. The following weekend, I arrived at their office and, after watching a couple of presentations made by the team, several things became apparent to me.

The organization was doing commendable work in its chosen field, though that does not necessarily preclude people's willingness to fund them. Be that as it may, they were going about their effort to reach out to people, mostly those who had funded them in the past or were friends, in the best way they knew. They wrote emails to prospective donors, attaching meticulously made presentation decks detailing their projects and their vision along with video testimonials of their achievements. Then they waited for the donors to respond. As it turned out, most did not, and the few that did were vague and non-committal.

At the core, the team was facing a number of classic sales problems.

What stood out the most for me was the improper segmentation of their prospects. They were mostly writing to people who were known to have money and, in some cases, to people who had made donations to charities before. What had missed their attention was the simple fact that they were chasing the easy picks, exactly those who were already being hounded by several other fund seekers. Many among them had founded their own charity organizations to enhance their personal brands. On top of that, such people had elaborate staff whose jobs entailed screening out emails that solicited money.

The basic question that the team hadn't applied their

mind to was: What is in the deal for the buyer? To crack this problem, the team would have to put themselves in the other person's shoes.

Once I had explained the problem to them, we put our heads together and it was decided that they would begin to remedy their situation by approaching a very different segment of prospects. Instead of approaching the donors who were already well-known for their wealth and charity, they would seek out a second tier of wealthy individuals who would consider associating with a charity aspirational, who might consider such an effort as adding to their brand value. The results were immediate, and very quickly my friend's organization was able to sign up a new set of donors.

Having tackled the issue of segmentation, we now attacked the aspect of reach. The team at the charity had assumed that emails were the right medium to get a 'yes' from potential donors. At best, an email can seek assent to a suggestion of receiving more information (permission marketing), or consent for a short phone call or a face-to-face meeting at a convenient time. It cannot, however, perform the complete process that seals the deal.

And this was just part of the problem. The big gripe with the team was the negligible responses they got to their emails. It was frustrating, they said in unison.

Here was another vital thing that no one had told the team

about: Even the greatest direct mail campaign by the best marketers in the world seldom yields more than a 4 per cent response rate. And a reply by no means equals a cheque. It can be anything from 'thank you, but no thanks' to 'call me next year' to 'send me more information' to 'let us meet after a month' to 'drop by next week'.

No one sends you a cheque because you sent an email.

My friends needed to make peace with the fact that the efforts they had made so far with the suspects were far smaller than what would yield them an adequate first set of interested prospects. In essence, they needed to widen their funnel. If you do not keep your funnel wide enough when you are prospecting, the trickle-down to the customers who will eventually buy from you will be equally limited. You are, after all, in the widest section of the funnel, with much more distance to travel and many more obstacles to encounter before you make the final sale.

Which brings me to one of nature's most exquisite marvels: the life-cycle of the coho salmon.

■

THE SALMON'S JOURNEY

If you do not keep your funnel wide when you are prospecting, the trickle-down to the customers who will eventually buy from you will be equally limited.

THE COHO SALMON IS one of the most prized fish in the world – both for game fishing and as food. Adult fish have their spawning grounds in fresh water – rivers, inland lakes and similar water bodies that are connected to the sea. This is where the adult males and females travel during the spawning phase of their lives; the females to leave their eggs, and the males to fertilize them. Not all eggs survive till hatching; many are eaten by other freshwater animals, some fall into unfavourable waters, still others are rendered unviable due to any one of the million natural hazards they encounter.

About a year after the eggs hatch, the baby fish, now known as smolts, leave their birthing waters and travel to the ocean.

This, again, is an arduous journey that many do not survive. The ones that do reach the open ocean mature and grow into adults. And then, in one of nature's most mysterious and wondrous turns, these new adults return one day to the fresh water in which they were born, to produce their own offspring. It is not certain how they recognize when it is time to spawn, but when they do, the fish make the same arduous journey back to fresh water, to the exact place of their birth, in order to continue the cycle. The adult fish die after spawning and 'nature's funnel' begins its work once more.

To put this into context, let's look at the following example in numbers.

Out of the 2,500 eggs that an adult coho salmon may lay, about 375 survive to hatch.

Of these 375 baby fish, most do not make it to the juvenile age. Only about 30 grow large enough to become smolts – juvenile salmon that are big enough to migrate into the ocean.

Of these 30 smolts that begin the journey to the ocean, only around five survive and flourish.

Of the 2,500 possible coho salmon that we started with, only about five make it to adulthood, and of those only two one day return to fresh water to spawn.

It is a sobering thought: *Spawned salmon have only a 1250:1 chance of becoming adults and spawning themselves.*

The ratio of the number of eggs to hatchling to smolt and, eventually, to adult salmon that make it back to the spawning ground can be likened to the ratio of customers at the various stages of selling, from prospecting to closing. Successful selling depends on salespeople knowing their funnel intimately. In other words, they need to know the conversion rate from potential customer to returning client, and how well (or poorly) the opportunities at hand are likely to be converted into actual business at any point in time.

Thankfully, in most businesses, the conversion rate between prospecting and closing is not as bleak as the salmon's egg-to-spawning adult rate of 1250:1. In selling, the ratio between landing a prospect to converting the opportunity to a sale is, at best, around 25:1.

While segmenting your customers is the first step, and casting your net wide among them is the second, the third essential consideration is knowing how to figure out who among the customers you've tapped is most likely to make an actual purchase and, more importantly, who will simply keep you hanging, give you the runaround or just prove to be a sheer waste of your time.

NO MONKEY BUSINESS, THIS

Qualifying a prospect is not always easy to do, but it is essential. Performing to the wrong audience can suck away time and energy like few other things can – and in the end you may find you have invested in a profitless endeavour.

A STREET PERFORMER, ALONG with his troupe – two monkeys and a dog – was resting under a tree on a hot summer afternoon. It hadn't been a particularly productive day. The foursome had gone from one village to another, only to find the audience sparse wherever they went. The few who had tossed coins into the performer's plate at the end of the show did so more out of affinity than appreciation. They had seen him do this before and knew he would come again.

The entertainment business is hard work. As the performer and his troupe sat listlessly in the shade, a small crowd gathered before them, watching them with curiosity and expectation. Nonetheless, the foursome made no effort to put up an act. After a while, a particularly enthusiastic man in the crowd spoke up.

'Now that you're here, why not show us a trick or two?' he asked.

The performer looked up, assessed the speaker in one quick glance and replied, '*Tel tambaku tera, dekh tamasha mera.*'

It was a rebuff.

Translated, the rustic statement meant, 'Bring oil and tobacco to the party, and I'll show you a trick or two.' (Oil and tobacco were precious commodities at the time this phrase was coined.)In short, it isn't a free world.

The performer had swiftly sized up the onlooker as someone who was curious, enthusiastic and perhaps even interested in his troupe's act but nonetheless simply a passer-by, hanging around in the hope of being entertained for free. In sales terms, the fellow was the kind of buyer who would have loved to buy what was on offer, but had no demonstrable ability to pay. In colloquial Hindi, this man was a *fatru*; not a *meherban, kadardan, saheban*, that is, someone who would part with good money in exchange for a good performance.

All salesmanship, like the show of the itinerant performer whose story I've just narrated, is a production. It requires organization and energy. It demands investment of time, effort, thought and intelligence. Performing to the wrong audience can suck away time and energy like few other things can – and, in the end, you may find you have invested in a profitless endeavour.

Being commercially successful requires the ability to size up the prospect. This is known as 'qualifying' the audience. It is not always easy to do, and sometimes even the sharpest in the field get carried away and mistake a *fatru* for a *meherban*.

That said, the *fatru* is not the only kind of buyer a salesperson needs to be wary of. There are others as well. Faux prospects, in fact, come in a variety of guises.

Take, for example, the **GREAT GIVER OF HOMEWORK**.

The first time you call upon this type, he looks very seriously at your merchandise and asks you pointed questions that establish his understanding of the product. Then, instead of being upfront and telling you that he doesn't have either the money or the authority to make a purchase, he asks you to build a 'proof of concept'. So you go running back to your R&D team, who then burn the midnight oil to produce the proof. When you return to the prospect, he tells you: 'Leave it on my desk. I am going for an off-site. I will come back and look at it.' Three weeks later, you reach out to him, he bounces you around a couple of times and then calls you with another problem.

'Isn't it at all possible to have the solar panels in the basement of the building? I am sure someone has done that somewhere. Imagine the huge savings in space if we could crack that!'

'Can your machine dye the individual strands of wool pink on one side and red on the other?'

'Can the rotor blade of the helicopter be below the cockpit and not above? Is that at all a technical possibility?'

'Can the ERP be customized to create a whirring sound in the earholes of my boss when he ignores my purchase request for more than 72 hours?'

Well, truth be told, everything is possible. However, the question is: Where is the cash going to come from? Before you go back to the client with all the answers, think of the performer under the tree. There is a lot of wisdom in the *tel* and *tambaku* story.

Then there is the **PATRON SAINT OF THOUGHT LEADERSHIP**.

This is the guy who almost made it to the role of chief technology officer (CTO) or chief intelligence officer (CIO) or chief financial officer (CFO) of the organization. He knows a thing or two and is probably an extremely well-read guy, but he is still someone who lacks business savvy and has therefore been 'parked' in his current post until the next reorganization. This person is a benign man. He misses the attention he doesn't get. He welcomes every visitor and gives each one as much time as he or she could ever want. He might even show up at your trade-show booth with sincere curiosity and impress you with his engineering brilliance and his vast knowledge about everything under the sun.

When you ask for his business card he readily obliges. Yet, over a series of follow-up calls – and there are many – you see that the distance between the Patron Saint of Thought Leadership and the cash that is essential for him to make that purchase is roughly the same as that between Heaven and Hell.

And how can I not talk about the **PERMANENT PROSPECT**?

This is someone who is always discussing a deal but will never *ever* close it. His name appears on your list as well as the list of all your competitors. They have met him many times over, as have you, but no deal ever seems to get sealed. In the 'sales funnel', a deal with this fellow will never graduate from one level to the next, and at the end of the day this prospect will always remain just that – a prospect.

Besides these, there is also the **POOR BRAHMIN**.

This is the well-meaning guy who badly needs what you are selling and will have real use for it, but offers his loincloth as guarantee for future payment. Your product costs ₹5,00,000. He has a budget of ₹50,000. He wants you to think of leaving your contraption as a 'demo unit', and promises that he and you could work on a breakthrough idea (it was he who had first thought of it twenty-three years ago and no one recognizes that, he will tell you) if your company could give him two engineers to work full-time alongside him. He has no doubt he will be able to develop a prototype and if his company doesn't buy the idea you could sell it to many others, and formulate a joint go-to-market strategy with him and get super rich.

To have the greatest product or service to sell is not enough. When selling a product, a service or an idea, you need to cut through the maze to locate the *real* prospects and shake hands with them. They alone are capable of becoming real customers. The path to that can sometimes be arduous, but if done well, qualifying a prospect accurately can lead to a great deal more.

In order to steer clear of the types described above and grab the guy who will bring both *tel* and *tambaku* to the show – that is, in order to qualify prospects – a salesperson needs to be a sharp observer, a good judge of people and their potential and be able to learn quickly from any instance of misjudgement they've made earlier.

Asking yourself a few quick questions to assess the person you're meeting will help:

Who is this person?

What is his real story?

How did he get here?

Is he the right guy to be talking to about this deal?

Is he competent?

Does he have organizational authority and authority over finances?

Is he a recommender, a buyer, a subject-matter expert, an influencer, the end user, or all of the above?

Is he self-appointed or anointed?

In watching salespeople at work, I have often found a certain reluctance to probe if the prospect is genuine. The best way to probe is to ask leading questions. But fear that the customer may feel offended, and sometimes false hope that the person you're meeting could be the one with the golden key, end up eating into the most precious asset of a salesperson: His time.

■

WHAT'S YOUR GQ?

Today's buyers are well-informed about the product and the seller, and the seller's Google Quotient (GQ) is a talking point. People don't like to buy from someone who is not special – because the one thing that has not changed is that people buy from people.

THE FLIGHT TO CHICAGO took longer than usual. I was stopping over in the Windy City on my way to New Jersey and had taken the opportunity to meet up with an old colleague of mine, a gentleman named Venkat Nandikola. Venkat was an alumni of the Indian Institute of Technology (IIT), Chennai, and the Xavier Institute of Management (XIM), Bhubaneswar. He had joined the IT industry early on and several years of hard work had taken him to the top rungs at Mindtree. He was one of the select set of people to have received the Chairman's Award for Excellence every year for several years for being an ace at his job.

I had, in part, decided to meet him to gather his take on the tricks of the trade, and had told him as much. Aside from the delay, the flight to Chicago had been uneventful and, after what seemed like an eternity, I finally got off the sky-bridge and walked down a long corridor to collect my baggage. A little while later, I was waving at Venkat, who was waiting for me at the arrival gate of the O'Hare International Airport. After a warm handshake, we walked out of the terminal right into the blast of cold winds from Lake Michigan; a harsh, but quintessentially Chicago welcome. Mercifully, the walk to the car was a short one and I was happy to jump in and slam the door shut. As he began to reverse out of the parking lot, I realized how clean Venkat's car was and complimented him on it. 'I never go out in a dirty car,' he replied. 'It follows another rule of mine: Always dress up; do not dress down.'

A bemused expression on my face, I exclaimed, 'Ah, so the lessons have begun!'

'The clean car theory extends to the boot, by the way,' he added. 'You never know when your backside is up for public viewing.' I grinned at the thought.

I found myself remembering my father's counsel when I was a little boy who owned just one pair of black shoes. He would tell me, 'Son, always keep those shoes shiny and clean. You never know who you will meet today. Your shoes will speak about the company you keep.' It appeared that Venkat had found a corollary that extended to his car. For the rest of the journey, we caught up on each other's lives – our families and work – and about forty-five minutes later, I checked into my room at the Marriot Midway Hotel.

The next morning, Venkat joined me for breakfast at the hotel before I headed to the airport and on to New Jersey. We resumed our conversation from the previous evening, with me gently prodding him to tell me about his experiences as a salesperson and the lessons he had gathered from his years of work. I was also curious about how things had changed in the industry from the time he had been a rookie salesperson. Today, he oversaw the work of many salespeople who considered him a wizard at his job and learnt from him how to weave magic.

'Many things remain the same, Subroto,' Venkat told me. 'The basic concept of selling, the need for it, the cycle – these haven't changed. What has changed is access to information. The Internet – it has changed the way we do things so much... Earlier only the seller had information. Today the buyer has as much and more. Earlier only the seller did the prospecting, today that isn't the case.'

'Ah, the prospect is also prospecting hard,' I heard myself say.

'Yes,' he laughed. 'In the good old days, I was pounding the streets and cold calls were always made in person. You know, cold calls were like blind dates. You never knew what would come up. That stuff has changed. It occurs to me that today more meetings, including cold calls, happen on the telephone or over live video streaming, and certainly on email.'

The server arrived at our table. 'Gentlemen,' she chimed, with sunshine in her voice, 'coffee or orange juice?' She had jugs of both in her hands. She looked like she was a freshman at a college. I greeted her cheerily before asking for some juice, while Venkat settled for coffee.

Taking a sip of his coffee, Venkat mulled over the thought further. 'Cold calls of the past were intrusive,' he said. 'When I was learning the ropes during my early days in India, you just landed up at the office of a prospect. Today, you have LinkedIn. You have the web. You do your pre-call research. Then you email the prospect or meet him or her at a trade show after setting up a convenient time.'

'That's true,' I agreed.

'Those days,' Venkat went on, 'the customer listened to your pitch for the first time and that is how you told them who you were. But today we have moved from cold calls to what I call "cold–warm" calls.'

'What are those?' I asked.

'Informed calls where you may be meeting your customer for the first time but both of you know enough about each other and the product on offer already,' he said. 'The email you've sent them ahead of your meeting has conveyed not only the essentials about the purpose of your call but that you have researched your prospect well... And one needs to watch out for shallow research. You can't fake it; the customer is way too smart and knowledgeable these days, with access to much more information on the product or you than ever before. People pick up on a phoney in an instant, and no one likes a pretender. You are better off saying, "I do not know anything about you and want to learn" than pretending that you're knowledgeable. And you can't forget that just as *you* have researched the prospect, so has the prospect researched you.'

The server returned; I asked for a three-egg garden omelette with no cheese while Venkat asked for a bowl of fruit. *Frugal choice*, I thought, considering my lavish one, but abandoned my thoughts on his diet since the conversation was taking a deep turn.

I told Venkat something I had learnt from one of the co-founders at Mindtree, Kalyan Banerjee, who now taught computer science at Centurion University back home, where he doubled up as the pro-vice-chancellor. Kalyan had spoken to me about how people research each other on the web. 'They are seeking to check your presence to know your capabilities,' Kalyan had said, 'not your company's, but *yours*.' He called it GQ – Google Quotient. 'If I Google you, what will show up on page one?' he had asked. 'Do you have a blog? Have you authored a point-of-view document? Is there a YouTube video that shows you teaching a bunch of college kids? If you don't have a GQ it means you are just a commodity. People don't like to buy from someone who is not special.'

'He's right,' agreed Venkat.

As he was about to continue, my omelette and his bowl of fruits arrived at the table and I found that I could no longer hold in my curiosity about his sparse breakfast.

'Is that all you will be eating? Dieting, are you?'

He dug into a piece of green melon and looked up.

'No way! I learnt something early on in the United States: Don't go to a serious meeting over breakfast without having eaten breakfast at home. You can't talk with food in your mouth. A breakfast meeting must be more meeting, less breakfast.'

He had a point there, but my omelette was here and there was just one place it was going!

Our conversation returned to the subject of engaging with a prospect. 'Even in the old days,' said Venkat, 'we had to qualify a prospect. We had to check all the boxes: Has need? Will buy? Can pay? Answering these questions calls for gut instinct. Today, this is almost entirely determined by data. Salespeople now need to build an affinity for data. They need to learn how to use data. I personally find the good old annual report of a client to be a veritable gold mine of information. But I pay particular attention to analysts' reports – both the trade analysts' and the financial analysts' – because they are able to frame a perspective based on a particular industry vertical to which the prospect may belong.'

The server arrived with the cheque and left it on the table with a cheery, 'No hurry, whenever you are ready.'

It was just about time for me to leave. I looked at the cheque left by the waitress, took out two $20 bills that would cover the charge as well as a 20 per cent tip and got up to leave. As we headed out I asked Venkat what *hadn't* changed from then to now.

He looked at me with the authority of a wizard and said, 'People buy from people. That hasn't changed.'

We shook hands and bade farewell to each other, and I headed out for my flight.

■

THE GRAIN HOUSE RESTAURANT

The best salespeople see themselves as consultants who can advise their clients and bring teams together to create a solution.

NOTHING APPEARED TO HAVE changed at the Grain House Restaurant in Basking Ridge, New Jersey, in eighteen years, which was how long it had been since I was last here. 'Well,' I told myself as I arrived for my dinner with Scott Staples, whom I was there to meet, 'the place has been here since the eighteenth century; what can change in eighteen years?'

In many ways, I was glad to see that nothing had changed. The place was special to me. It was where I first met Scott Staples and pitched the idea of Mindtree to him. I was 'selling' him the idea of building something together. It had been our first meeting, one that came about on the recommendation of Anjan Lahiri, who had already signed up to co-found

Mindtree. We wanted a hot-rod sales guy who would land us big deals, and we had identified Scott. Scott, of course, doesn't see himself as a salesperson – and for good reason – but more on that later.

Scott had grown up in a typical middle-class American household. His mother was a school teacher and his father, a military pilot. Like most American children, he grew up doing odd jobs in the neighbourhood to supplement his allowance. One such gig was as a window-cleaner. He loved his work because, as he put it, 'You could see the impact of your work immediately, while you're doing it.' It also taught him the importance of doing a job perfectly. In the window-cleaning business, if you didn't do it right, it was obvious; there was no way to hide a dirty patch left behind on glass.

When we met at the Grain House that first time, Scott was working with Cambridge Technology Partners, where he and Anjan sold business solutions. Scott had confessed to being unhappy with his work. The business solutions he sold often did not deliver on the promises he made to his clients. The organization wasn't geared towards servicing clients with what was being offered on paper. It left a bitter taste in many mouths and caused rancour, and Scott knew that a continuing association with such an organization would damage his reputation as a professional.

I, on the other hand, was in search of someone like him,

who really believed in his work and would do what was required to make the customer massively successful. At the end of our first dinner at the Grain House, Scott and I shook hands. 'We have a deal,' he said as he signed up.

What ensued were years of great partnership and, over time, my admiration for him grew immensely. Today, Scott runs Mindtree's business in the United States. He has many salespeople working with him, selling solutions to our clients.

This evening, our dinner was unhurried.

My conversation with Venkat in Chicago had got me thinking and I had warned Scott that we may spend much of our time talking shop. Diving right in, I asked Scott much the same question that I had asked Venkat. How had selling changed from the time when he had begun as a rookie salesperson fresh from college?

'Digital,' said Scott concisely. 'It's all digital now.'

'That sounds like a cliché to me,' I replied.

'No, no,' he said with authority. 'Let me give you an analogy: In the old days, gold prospectors would not know if a river had large gold deposits as compared to another river. They simply had to get into the water and start panning the sediment to determine the river's potential. Today, gold prospectors can use geological mapping technologies, rock assay analysis, and so on to determine ahead of time whether prospecting a specific river location is worth the effort. This is similar to how prospecting is done today – with LinkedIn, RainKing, individual company websites, online annual reports and so on.

'But, even with all of this science,' he continued, 'half of prospecting is still an art.'

The 'art', he explained, lay in being able to take all of the data and determine the opportunities that existed in specific industries. In other words, with the data at hand, a salesperson's task was to identify the inefficiencies or 'pain points' in an ailing company and then approach those companies with specific solutions. Good prospectors would, in addition, also know how to form and communicate simple, hard-hitting messages to pique the client's interest.

'I believe there are thousands of salespeople who can win deals,' Scott said, 'but there are only hundreds among them who can *find* the deals that can be won. The "finding" is actually the hard part, and good prospecting and cold calling approaches are needed for it to be done well. The salespeople who do this are the ones who walk on water.'

Scott was now in full flow. 'Like the mainframe of the computer hardware business, cold calling will never go away, but it is a legacy approach to reaching someone. In the analogue days, there was a concept called the "golden hour", the time when the executives were at their desks with no admin to screen incoming calls – generally before 9.00 a.m. and after 7.00 p.m. That was the perfect window for cold calling. In the digital age, prospects want to interact electronically, but there still has to be a certain percentage of old-fashioned cold calling because people will open up and communicate more once you get them on the phone. Today's approach has to be a multi-media approach: LinkedIn connections, emails, cold calling, networking at events and conferences, and so forth. To be a good business development manager you would have to use a mix of all of these to try and land an account.'

'The golden hour cold call may still work to some degree, but people don't work like this any more. Executives are always connected, always on the move, and hard to reach. You have to be smart about when to reach out. As an example, an email sent on a Monday morning is a waste of time. When do executives have the most emails piled up? Monday morning. Since executives are usually tied to their smartphones, the best time to send emails is late in the evening, when you are hoping to catch them flipping through their phone while travelling somewhere, or on a weekend, when there are hardly any emails coming in and they are looking leisurely at their phones.'

I nodded, fascinated at how the older methods had been adjusted around the changes new technologies had brought forth.

Scott paused to take a bite of his meal, and I sipped at my water as I thought about what he was saying. 'So, is it better or worse, in your opinion?' I asked. 'Have all the technological advancements made life easier or harder?'

'Well, in one respect the analogue days were better,' admitted Scott, putting down his fork. 'The new age salesperson relies too much on public information and can even forget to ask clients basic questions. Digital information can be a crutch and often, the basic tenets of Sales 101 are forgotten. I mean, you could do all the research you want but if you want to know how your client organization functions in relation to purchasing your product, you'd have to address the necessary questions directly to your client. Say, you have to know how the purchase will be funded or who in particular will be involved in the decision-making process or even how long it will take to make a choice and issue a purchase order – you'll have to do the asking. No software or database can give you that.'

'So one has to remember that a tool is a tool, and not the process?' I said, summing up his point of view.

'Yes, that's right. But there's more to the story. I strongly believe that the best salespeople do not see themselves as salespeople,' replied Scott firmly. 'The best salespeople see themselves as consultants who can advise their clients, bring teams together to create a solution, and finally sell that solution with a consultative approach. Someone that says their job is in "sales" is probably not a consultative seller. When you go to a doctor and fill out a patient form, there is always a question about occupation. The best salespeople will not write "sales" in that box. They will write "consultant".'

'Or perhaps "window cleaner",' I said in jest.

Scott laughed out loud. 'Yes, you could say that...' he said with a twinkle in his eye.

■

THE MAGIC EQUATION

Familiarity with a client is a competitive strength. The most important thing is your chemistry with your customer. If that is not in place, you won't succeed.

I HAVE KNOWN VIKRAM Kaul for a long time now as a salesperson who has worked his way up the ladder – from being an individual professional contributor to running a very large part of his company's business in the United States. Even as Vikram became the big boss, he never gave up his primary profession and has remained a trusted advisor to his clients. Among the many qualities that make him successful, there is one that I find most interesting: The way he uses trade shows to get prospects – so much so that I call him the 'Trade Show King'. These days, more and more business gets done at trade shows, ranging from real estate to defence armaments, garden implements to kitchen appliances.

Why do I call Vikram the 'Trade Show King'? Because

he knows how to make the most of trade shows to strike a business deal. One of the many reasons for his success is that, for Vikram, the planning begins long before the actual opening of a show! He first chooses very carefully the shows he wants to attend by identifying where his customers go to buy, sell and network. A couple of months in advance, he begins to track the sponsoring companies – all of them, from the platinum down to the gold and silver sponsors – and researches the executives of these companies. He then writes to them individually, personalizing his message to both introduce himself and tell them very briefly about what he does. He follows up on these emails by asking for a meeting. By the time the show begins, Vikram ensures that he has also found out all he needs to know about the advisory firms for the show, the speakers at various sessions and, of course, the exhibitors.

In essence, he joins the dots and creates a complete and comprehensive mental image of the trade show weeks before it is scheduled to begin. That is a lot of work considering that he attends as many as sixteen or seventeen trade shows a year. Add four days to that for travel, an extended stay for meetings and the rest, and it works out to a third of the working days in a year, more or less. That is how Vikram creates opportunities to sell.

According to Vikram, the process of selling is transforming

itself into a three-step process. It is about connecting, educating and engaging. And, through it all, it is about trust. Customers are looking for trust.

'Once, I learnt a nice formula for trust at a training programme I attended. The programme was being run by Korn Ferry – you know...' said Vikram.

I nodded. 'The HR (human resources), leadership and recruitment folks?'

'Yes, those guys,' he continued, possibly wishing for a stronger reaction from me. 'The formula is this...' he said, raising his eyebrows portentously to indicate the true value of the insight he was about to share with me. With his fingers he wrote in the air while he mouthed the words: 'Trust is equal to Familiarity multiplied by Expertise, divided by Risk.'

Trust = (Familiarity × Expertise) / Risk

It seemed both sensible and workable; one's expertise is always a positive contribution when making a sale, as is familiarity with the client. And risk is always the divisive factor.

Impressed, I said, 'Tell me this: Expertise I understand, but how do you increase familiarity before you've even met your clients?'

'Through preparation,' he said firmly. 'The preparation that you do ahead of time. You have to be more familiar with the customer than your competition. Familiarity is a competitive strength. No, you can't do it through LinkedIn alone. Go beyond that when you research an organization. Read the analyst briefings on the company, watch the videos of their key executives on YouTube. Pay attention to the pauses and read between the lines. When you meet them at a trade show, ask them about their requirements. Let them speak while you remain silent; listen deeply.

'In sales,' Vikram continued, drawing a deep breath, 'you need to focus on three things: physics, chemistry and maths. Physics is the matter, the form and function, the price of what you sell. Chemistry is the relationship you build with the customer. And maths is your revenue and profit targets and that comes from what the customer pays you. In this triad, it is chemistry that is the most important. If that is not in place, you won't succeed, the other two notwithstanding.'

Indeed, I thought, my mind going back to a particular deal in which, due to inadequate validation of the customer's requirement, what we delivered to the customer was not what they had wanted. But thanks to the longstanding chemistry between the teams at both ends, the customer did not get into a blame game and gave us another chance to get it right. In contrast, countless examples abound in every organization, and well beyond sales as well, where the wrong chemistry has brought about the downfall of many a good product, great pricing notwithstanding.

But the trick is to balance it all perfectly, right, I asked myself.

As though he had read my mind, Vikram said, 'Well, Subroto... Increase the chemistry to improve the physics to deliver the maths. And there you have it!'

■

AND THE DOG'S NAME IS...

Customers love weirdness - if you have it, don't ever lose it. In fact, use it.

IF THERE IS ONE man I know who has always demanded that salespeople deliver Vikram's chemistry–physics–maths equation, it is Bill Eggleston.

Bill is a hefty man with a booming voice, who is both gregarious and somewhat playfully belligerent. He has a sharp wit; his humour lashes forth like lightning and can be cutting, but he doesn't spare himself either. He is constantly seeking opportunities to negotiate and believes that deal-making is the primal dharma of all creation. Bill loves to talk about his law degree at the University of Pennsylvania, of having co-authored a voluminous textbook that paid him handsomely, of having worked in many countries before joining SITA (Société Internationale de Télécommunications

Aéronautiques), a consortium of airline companies that builds technology solutions for air transport companies. Bill's job is that of contract management. Anyone wanting to close a deal with SITA must go past Bill. I have known Bill for more than a decade, and I admire his energy and zest for life as much as his ability to surprise people, which is infinite. He is French by origin and mother tongue; American in his head; works out of Geneva, negotiates contracts in every part of the world; and perennially wants to escape to a farmhouse somewhere in Belgium.

I recall a particular day in Geneva when, after a hard day of business negotiations, while driving to a Lebanese restaurant in his convertible, he turned up the music and began to sing a soulful Sufi song in his bellowing voice. He wasn't particularly melodious, but his effort won me over. Turning towards me – the sole passenger in the car – he asked me to name the singer, fully expecting that I would not be able to do so. This once, however, I did know the answer, and he was both surprised and pleased because a Pakistani singer not related to Bollywood is a tough guess for most. The perpetual deal-maker, Bill offered me a prize on the spot.

It was my turn to cash in, and I asked him to come to London to address some of my business development people on the fine art of selling. In my opinion, his point of view is invaluable, for he knows the world of salesmanship from the vantage point of negotiating large contracts on behalf of SITA.

In London, Bill arrived for the talk with a bunch of slides (which, truth be told, he didn't really need). He arrived well before his talk was scheduled to begin, picked up a coffee during the break, chuckled and growled and guffawed his way through opening conversations with the people in the room and though someone or the other was constantly at the receiving end of his jokes the interaction was playful and good-natured.

Then it was show time.

He began with his usual belligerence, challenging the audience.

'Anyone know what SITA stands for… Anybody?'

There was discomfort and silence for the most part, because those in the room had not dealt with that particular account. As it turned out, many people didn't even know it was an acronym and had assumed that SITA was the organization's actual name.

A bold hand went up. A brave soul knew the answer. I let out a sigh of relief from the far end.

'Société Internationale de Télécommunications Aéronautiques,' he offered.

But Bill wasn't impressed. He asked the fellow who had answered to tell everyone how the name was pronounced in

French. The poor guy looked trapped. As the awkward silence went on, Bill looked incredulous.

'Salespeople,' he boomed at the intimidated lot before him, 'need to know everything – *everything* – about their customers. You've got to know the name of your customer's dog!' he barked.

After a spilt second, the audience burst into appreciative laughter at the audacity of Bill's goal. He had caught them off-guard, and that too with an unassuming line. However, it got me thinking. I realized that despite knowing Bill for years, I had never bothered to ask him his dog's name. I made a mental note to do so as soon as I got him alone.

What followed was an intense session covering a number of aspects crucial to bringing more efficiency to the selling process. I submerged myself in it along with the others in the room.

Bill began on a strong note. 'The most important thing,' he said, 'is not to take yourself too seriously. Customers like to deal with and buy from people who are comfortable being themselves. People who don't feel guilty about who they are. If you are in this job, you aren't stupid. So go ahead and enjoy it.'

Someone asked Bill a profound question. 'Everyone,' he said, referring to salespeople in the services business, 'is smart. Everyone goes through sales and account management and negotiation skills, and all the other training programmes. And everyone, more or less, has good products to offer. If you aren't good, you aren't in the final shortlist anyway. So, how do you stand apart?'

Bill's response was immediate. 'In this world, there are way too many ME TOOs – too many companies, products, services and people. You have to project to your customer what sets you apart. Customers love weirdness – if you have it, don't ever lose it. In fact, *use it*!'

The audience nodded, looking a little unsure, while I revelled in Bill's ability to hit the nail so roundly on the head. There was a time when everyone talked about things like unique selling proposition (USP) and differentiation. Buyers would ask what is special about your product. But, today, we live in a world in which everyone is cloning everyone else. The relatively permanent difference doesn't come from a unique product or service. It comes from 'weirdness' – the magical, attractive, attention-grabbing capability of the people (read: company) behind the product. The Tatas are weird. Apple is weird. Facebook is weird. Weird is ahead of its time. Weird is good.

'Sometimes,' Bill resumed, turning tack quite suddenly, 'people inherit customer relationships. This happens more with account managers who take on an existing relationship. Inherited customers come as a mixed bag. Some can be really tricky, some can be messed up. There could well be contracts that you abhor dealing with. It's like the good old saying: Success has many fathers, failure is a bastard.'

The audience nodded sagely, while Bill swung around to the white board behind him, filling it with words written in big, bold letters:

OVER-PROMISE (you) / OVER-EXPECTATION (customer) UNDER-DELIVER

'All of these things can lead to a contract getting screwed up. So,' he growled as he scribbled on, surprising everyone in the room, 'if you get one of those, whosoever it may have belonged to earlier, OWN IT!' He underlined the last word on the board about five times:

OWNERSHIP

'You will need to look at two things: The length of the relationship and its future value. That exercise is like lifting yourself from the street-view of a building to the satellite view. Be resourceful. Take some, give more. Be done with it, move on. You will be respected for it forever,' he finished.

The audience sat, silent, considering the nugget of wisdom Bill had just dropped, quite vehemently, in their collective lap.

By the time the session approached its end, everyone was in awe of Bill. But I had something more to ask him...

As I left Bill's session that evening, I walked across to the tube for the Circle Line towards Kensington High Street with a spring in my step. The train pulled in, and when the doors opened, I got in and took the same vacant seat I took every day. Once in there, I settled back, happy that I now knew the names of Bill's canine and feline family members: Simba and Nala.

■

NAVIGATING THE ARCTIC ICE

Deal-making can be a complex process. A good player maps all the stake-holders, guages their role in the negotiation process, and then watches the ice carefully for any untoward movements.

VIKRAM SRIVATS, A TALL, lanky man with the demeanour of a scientist, doesn't come across as someone who works in sales at all. Yet that is what he really does. He sells Bluetooth™ licences to electronics manufacturers of all kinds, that is, those who make ear-phones, headsets, medical equipment and navigational devices that sit on an automobile's dashboard. Sometimes he sells technology licences to semi-conductor companies who, in turn, embed the technology onto their chips. These deals are complex, to say the least; many of them take months at a time to close.

Selling intellectual property to a customer who will then embed it in their equipment involves dealing with multiple organizations within the client's organization. You don't sell to one person; you sell to many. You don't sell to just one department, you sell to many. Often it gets so complex that Vikram describes the selling process as he experiences it as 'navigating the Arctic ice'.

'Navigators on ships traversing the Arctic,' he tells me, speaking about his work, 'which has dense ice packs that often hide mountains of rock within, must have very special skills. They need to chart the course and map the terrain; else, they run the risk of getting lost and, sometimes, end up sinking. Client organizations are often like that. You can't stumble once you're in there. You have to navigate constantly. You must be able to map the influence of the people in the organization – both the formal structure that is visible above the surface, and the shadow structure below it. Without that, you will get nowhere.'

'But surely a navigator in the Arctic has a much more difficult task than a salesperson?' I asked, somewhat sceptical of his view. 'Deal-making is not such a complicated process, is it, Vikram?'

'Every deal,' Vikram explained with the patience of a kindergarten teacher, 'has at least eight different people influencing it. The person you are interacting with directly is just one of them. A good player maps all the stakeholders, identifies their personal motivations, gauges what their end game might be, and what they know and appreciate of what the seller is trying to bring to the table.'

Vikram went on to talk about the stakeholders in deals that he was most familiar with – the ones that a salesperson negotiating a large deal will necessarily encounter. I imagine that even if in different avatars, depending on the industry they work in, salespeople will inevitably encounter the stakeholders that Vikram spoke of.

The Vendor Selection Expert.

On large deals, this is sometimes the first point of contact for a seller. A seasoned salesperson, of course, would have done his homework well in advance, moving upstream as compared to the other players. Don't lose heart the first time you find your way forward being blocked by this individual. The trick is to act quickly. Play innocent and suck in as much information as you can before you give anything away. In a large deal, often the vendor selection expert's job is to knock out a long list of potential suppliers, narrowing it down from a long to a short list. His job is to qualify a few suppliers without bias and give them the request for information (RFI) document. Once filled in, this document gets further scrutinized and then the list is shortened to a smaller group of potential suppliers who get a request for proposal (RFP). As one among many potential suppliers, your job is to please the vendor selection expert enough for him to tell you about things that are not part of the RFI document but will be crucial to your deal. He will be the one to tell you why a business opportunity is on the table. It could be a new CEO with a new agenda or an old contract coming to an end and put on bid. He'll also tell you what the broader selection criteria are, the dos and the don'ts beyond the regular terms and conditions you should know about when engaging with the particular organization, and he'll answer the most crucial question: Who is the buyer?

The Buyer.

The most obvious player, the buyer is the person who needs your product or service. This person will probably have the most say in the deal, but must also listen to the advice of others. In very large deals, the buyer may not be the end user; nonetheless, he represents their interests and opinions. In large deals at big corporations, the buyer, even though he is the most important player, may arrive late at the scene. The other players may create a short-list prior to his arrival. Whether or not this is the case, one has to know about the buyer's past, present and future in as much detail as possible.

The External Expert.

The buyer sometimes has an external expert to assist in decision-making. This person is usually a consultant from a specialized firm and knows both the technological aspects of the product being considered as well as the many ways that the deal can be structured. They lead with knowledge and reputation. They have been there and done that with previous clients. These are the people you must flood with all the white papers at your disposal, so that you come across as being at the cutting-edge of your business. You must also be able to give them the assurance that you will protect their reputation if they recommend you.

The Influencer.

These are people who often wield a great deal of authority over the deal even though they may not be the buyer or the user. These could be people from the corporate office, for example, or the Quality team whose opinion it is difficult to override. Sometimes, though, they might try to influence the deal in odd ways. For example, the chief financial officer (CFO) of a prospective firm might ask if, as part of the deal, you would be open to buying some old unused iron they have in stock. Or an HR head might want people to be rebadged and taken on employee rolls as part of an outsourcing deal. Or it could be a director wanting to know whether you would be open to a build-own-operate-transfer kind of arrangement. These people are almost always people. They may not always speak when you meet the entire group together, but it is always good to keep a keen eye on their body language.

The Detractor.

This is someone who has fundamental – and sometimes fundamentalist – objections to the overall strategy behind the deal you are offering. It could be someone with a low opinion of your firm, or the product or service you bring to the table. Such people can wield unusual levels of authority, especially when there is a change of guard in the middle of the deal process. Say, for example, when the old CTO, who was a believer in outsourcing, is replaced by a new one who believes that the firm should actually be relying on in-house capabilities. This is a person who is not anti-you but anti-the solution you offer. Sometimes, the detractor is simply someone who favours your competitor, because they worked together in the former's previous company or some such. Even though you may not want to engage directly with this person, it is critical not to confuse him with a friend.

The Coach.

People who play this role are often silent and remain invisible; a good salesperson will make sure to search hard and identify him early on. The coach is often reclusive. This is the one person who has organizational memory. Usually, he is a part of the evaluation process, and knows a great deal about the formal and shadow structure of decision-making at the firm. He is someone able enough to recommend how much time you should spend on a particular department, and give you tips on what you should or shouldn't say, or perhaps even offer advice on when and how much to give in. He can show you the paw prints in the jungle where the big cats of competition are prowling. This man expects nothing from you other than respect, careful attention, periodic reports on what was done with his advice – the results – and, of course, loyalty.

The Competition.

The jungle, they say, has eyes. These eyes see you even as you don't see them. Sharpest among the watching eyes are those of your competition. You must know them all; the obvious ones as well as the not-so-obvious ones. (Always assume that there is something or someone that you have overlooked.) Know the antecedents of your competition. Identify the key individuals from the competition in the fray. You should know as much as you can about these people, else you risk losing the deal even before you begin. You should know their past wars, their motives; you should be able to anticipate their moves and also predict what they may be thinking about you.

The Lawyer.

This person is the king of the master agreement. To some he is a bloodsucker, a leech and an extortionist; to others he is a friend and a guide. Do not be afraid. Lawyers are human beings; at times they can be unexpectedly helpful and even have good jokes to tell. Increasingly, the role of the lawyer is evolving to protect the deal, not just the client. The best way to deal with a lawyer is to make sure you do your homework well and have a basic understanding of the legal aspects of your business.

'Each of these actors may come and go based on the script and flow of events,' Vikram said. 'In the end, it is a small group that decides; usually, this group must contain the buyer, the guy in charge of purchasing and the money man who takes the final call.'

'Last but not the least,' he continued, 'you must also know who handles the payments. This person may not be located in any of the offices you have visited so far; it may even be a machine. But if you don't identify this player correctly – and early on – your invoices will usually end up getting horribly stuck. Worse, the previous actors you had mapped until now will undoubtedly plead helplessness; in the absolute worst case, they may simply move on to the next deal.'

'Is there any good news in all of this?' I asked Vikram, somewhat jokingly. 'Isn't there someone who's interested in the deal for the *sake* of the deal? Someone who doesn't have a personal agenda?'

Vikram grinned. 'Yes,' he replied. 'At the end of this long list of individuals comes the sponsor. This is the KING or the QUEEN, as the case may be, whose grand idea has spawned the initiative that has brought about the current deal. This individual is the organization's leader who lives for legacy and nothing else. This individual may have no role to play in the mundane stuff, but before the final signing ceremony, they will be briefed; never underestimate their knowledge of and appetite for detail. If you can, while giving a hefty discount at the end, ask for a photo opportunity with them as part of the barter. It works wonders for the client testimonial page on your company's website.'

After the great conversation with Vikram about navigating the Arctic ice while mapping a deal on the table, I paused to reflect on why some people do so well as account managers, whether they work in technology companies or handle banking relationships with a client or sell real estate services to large corporations. It's because they know two things very well, I concluded:

First, that clients can be fickle and relationship-switching doesn't take as long as it did in the olden days. There is always your competition standing by with orders to 'take the mess for less'.

Second, even if a client isn't thinking of switching, it is much more cost-effective to do repeat business than to acquire new clients.

Effective client mapping is a great insurance against the eventuality of being dropped and it is a solid investment in the future value of a relationship.

It pays to know who is who even after you have won the deal. Some people do it well during the negotiation process but become careless later about acquiring updated information and maintaining relationships. As a result, they risk losing important business opportunities because they do not, intentionally or by discipline, continuously map the account. This is ever so critical because the Arctic ice is constantly changing. It is constantly forming and reforming and shifting. It is dynamic. It takes no time for a sponsor to hear about a botched deal (never mind who botched it) and dump you. A coach may move on, a detractor could take on the role vacated by the coach and guillotine you, and an influencer can feel that you aren't looping her in enough after you've landed the deal and therefore distance herself.

Sophisticated supplier organizations literally pay thousands of dollars to learn from consultants how to map an account and constantly monitor it through colour-coded heat maps of who is currently 'green', 'yellow' or 'red', based on interactions and feedback from the immediate past quarter. The colour coding is a function of several health parameters like business executed or lost, negotiations underway and their prognosis, opportunities in the funnel and, above all, reported customer satisfaction levels.

These organizations ask all the 'why' questions. Why have revenues risen or fallen compared to the previous quarter? Why were we invited or not invited to receive a particular request for proposal or submit a tender or make a pitch or an offer? Why did the customers escalate a system failure all the way up to the CEO? Why has the CEO of the client organization given us good ratings in the last satisfaction survey while the line managers who receive the goods and services dropped their ratings? Every 'why' leads to more questions until the root causes come up.

Based on their conclusions from this periodic, planned review, they make sure that the greens are being stoked, the yellows move to green and the reds either move to yellow or drop off, if the reason is strong enough. If the latter comes about then they must ensure that the transition is managed well so that there are no hard feelings at the clients' end. At the same time, they must engage in a thorough root-cause analysis, without ignoring the smallest of details. Timely evaluation of gaps, failings and mistakes – whether they are product, services or personality related – will go a long way in avoiding choppy waters in the future and, if such circumstances do arise, make negotiating them easier.

■

WHAT'S THE DEAL?

The negotiation process is like an elegant dance movement, where the customer and the seller are required to step in perfectly coordinated moves, each drawing the other in and taking it forward.

EVERY SALESPERSON OPENS HIS mailbox in the morning with two prayers: 'May there be a congratulatory message for a deal won' and 'May there be three mails at least with serious sales enquiries'. The previous successful deal, as any good seller knows, is already in the past. The future pipeline depends on the number of sales leads, RFPs or tenders one is working on at present.

Usually a tremendous amount of time needs to be devoted to working on leads, each one being equally demanding and exhausting. In fact, they demand the time and energy of many people in the organization apart from the salesperson. Good salespeople, therefore, often say no to certain types of leads that may not be worth the effort and can be a distraction in terms of time and energy. It is like choosing your play and playing it well.

What do we mean by 'playing it well'? The question reminded me of a description my colleague Bala Balachandran, a very successful account manager at Mindtree, had once used for the deal-making process between a customer and a seller. In Bala's words: 'Think of it as an elegant dance movement, where the customer and the seller are required to step in perfectly coordinated moves, each drawing the other in and taking it forward.'

My conversations with Bala had always yielded nuggets of wisdom. I had once asked Bala about the cardinal principles of managing a sales lead. Albeit, the discourse that ensued was strictly related to the selling of products that Bala was most acquainted with – IT services – but to me it was a collector's session that could be applied by any professional to a product or solution.

Treat each deal as if it's your first.

You may have worked on a similar deal and delivered a hefty set of negotiation terms to client A, but simply passing off the same terms and conditions to client B, no matter how similar they may seem to you, can be disastrous. Salespeople often lose sight of this when selling to existing clients. They settle into a rut, in a manner of speaking, and that is the first sign of rot in the customer–seller relationship. It is like a marriage that is slowly going downhill. The trick is to treat each proposal-making process as seriously as your first date. You just cannot take your partner for granted.

Take charge of delivering a complete package.

Unlike earlier times, more and more deals today require not just a point solution but a complete package. The customer wants you to put the pieces together even if you don't sell them. They prefer those who take complete charge. Therefore, your partnership network with those who provide services related to your product matters a lot. That is why, before anything happens, even before a lead comes through, you must consider the best partnerships possible for pitching your product. You have to show how you can take on and manage formidable tasks, the ones with many different aspects to them. The additional value you offer your client shows not just your expertise in the overall deal, but also your ability for extreme collaboration.

Bring the customer into the solutioning process.

Clients come in all shapes and sizes. Some may be tired of monotony and looking to do things differently; others may be genuinely ambitious and eager to prove to their organization that they can generate new, breakthrough ideas and have the ability to execute them. Under such circumstances, you need to bring something exciting to the table and be a co-creator of innovation. You need to show the client more than just half-baked ideas; you need to show them the 'proof of concept' you have built. This has to be something that assures your client beyond doubt that you can take your ideas to the next level; that you can genuinely create the next best-practice, and not just help them adopt the techniques that their competitors may already be using. Sometimes, innovation is an organizational imperative. It is, of course, a complex matter in a business-to-business environment because your customers are innovating in order to serve *their* customers better. In these cases, one important thing to think of is this: *Who is the customer's customer?* That piece of the iceberg is under the waterline. If you can reach out, understand the hidden needs and keep those in mind as you build a solution for the client you are bound to be seen as innovative and your proposal is bound to get the thumbs-up.

Think about the customer's risks.

Your customers live in an increasingly volatile world. In fact, as someone put it, these days there is a high probability that a low-probability occurrence will happen. You need to guard against possible risks, however unlikely they may be. There are no happy camping grounds in today's world of business.

Given this kind of volatility, customers like their vendors, suppliers or service providers to proactively think of the risks – especially those they might not have considered themselves – and suggest how they may be accounted for. This shows care and concern. It shows you are truly invested in the customer's success and not just in winning the deal.

Present a human face at each step of the interaction.

If you bought a new air-conditioning system at a hardware store, you would want to know who'd install it, wouldn't you? When you hail an Uber, you feel reassured when you know the name of the driver, his phone number and what he looks like. It is no different in business-to-business industries. The customer will want to know who the project manager is going to be when they give you the deal to revamp their website. If you are awarded the overall contract to build a new bridge across the bay, the customer will want to know who the key people will be for every aspect of the job. At each step, it is about the individuals. As Bala put it, 'Customers need to see the names on the back of the jersey.'

Make it visual.

This is the wave of the future – to go visual. Clients like to see what your proposed solution will look like. They don't want to read a lengthy, wordy proposal that is like a weed-infested garden – all text and numbers; they want to see screenshots and mock-ups. Physiologically, the brain gets the message faster when you 'see' something. Everyone likes to see in colour, smell actual smells, hear real sounds. In short, it is important to provide your customers with an immersive experience of the difference your product will make to their work and lives. Provide models, create manuals, build prototypes and mock-ups, use simulations using Augmented Reality and Virtual Reality (AR/VR) technology that is so commonly available today. Gaining the customer's trust, in you and the product, is the ultimate goal. Once that is done, the signature on the dotted line is a mere formality.

■

THE
NAKED
HAMBURGER

Believe in the value of the product you're delivering and then persuade the customer to believe in your perception.

M Y FIRST ENTREPRENEURIAL VENTURE was Project.21 back in 1985. Project.21 had been set up to train large corporations how to introduce and use desktop computers in their offices. We did a good job of it and, as the reputation of our small, twenty-person team grew, it led to continuous consulting assignments of this and other kinds. One such assignment was to help a company called Raba Contel sell, or should I say resell, its services to Apple.

At the time, Raba Contel was the exclusive distributor for Apple in the Indian subcontinent. You may recall Steve Jobs's early fascination with calligraphy. Apple was at the time the de-facto standard for what was known as desktop publishing and, therefore, Raba Contel had a monopoly position in the

Indian market. Even so, their founder and chief executive officer (CEO), Rakesh Gandhi, felt that they needed to reinvent their relationship with the iconic company because they had hit a plateau. This was nothing unusual. However good partnerships may be, as time progresses, they may well become stale. This can be the dangerous point at which relations start to sour, often invisibly and thus imperceptibly. From here on, matters invariably go south. The key is to think strategically and reinvent the relationship.

Thanks to Sunil Agarwal, a mutual friend and Rakesh's business advisor, Project.21 was roped in to recommend a strategic shift for Raba Contel vis-à-vis their association with Apple and I found myself presenting our recommendations to Rakesh. He was preparing to make a pitch to the Apple management at Apple's forthcoming sales conference at Club Med on the Malaysian coast, off the Red China Sea, and asked me to join him there. I doubted very much that I could add any further value (usually, consultants tend to repeat themselves after the first round of advisories), but the allure of the Red China Sea was overwhelming and I tagged along.

For the most part, it turned out to be a client-funded holiday for me. But the one thing that has stuck in my memory is a presentation made by Apple's global head of sales at that conference. To this day, every bit of what he said is embedded firmly in my head.

The title of his presentation was 'The Naked Hamburger', and this was the sum and substance of it:

A hamburger is not a complicated dish to prepare – two pieces of bun, a piece of meat, a lettuce leaf, some mayo, a slice or two of freshly cut onion rings and tomatoes, and perhaps a slice of cheese, put together in the easiest way possible – a kind of a stack. Nothing that you couldn't make yourself, with ingredients that can be found in any market. There is no rocket science to how hamburgers are made; none at all. However, if it is all that simple, why aren't a whole lot of other burger chains running McDonald's out of business? Why is McDonald's the world's No. 1 burger company, with 2016 global sales in excess of 24 billion, more than 36,000 restaurants across the world, and over 375,000 employees? What makes McDonald's so popular?

The answer is in the burger itself. McDonald's is McDonald's because they don't serve naked hamburgers. If you go to a McDonald's anywhere in the world, you are guaranteed a uniform product and service quality. This extends to the taste of the food, the décor of its outlets, the queuing time at each store, the cleanliness and maintenance of hygiene across stores – *everything*. What makes this possible is the huge amount of domain knowledge the company possesses, which includes tools, methodology, quality-control systems, innovation and branding. Every time you or I go to McDonald's, we are handed a small piece of all those things. Without those aspects, they would just be selling naked hamburgers.

Anyone can build a naked hamburger but no one has been able to achieve the ability that McDonald's has to deliver a predictable, familiar experience, every single time. That's why they are McDonald's.

Before you start wondering why the global sales head at Apple was hard-selling McDonald's at an Apple sales conference, let me fill you in on the background. As everyone knows, Apple products are not – and never were – cheap. In fact, at the time of this conference they were very expensive. Word processing was just taking off and word processors running on cheaper PCs (like those produced by IBM, Apple's arch-enemy in the personal computer business at the time) were beginning to cast a doubt in customers' minds as to why they should pay such hefty prices for Apple's dedicated desktop publishing machines which dominated the professional printing market. This was, in turn, beginning to affect the confidence of the frontline salespeople in Apple, who had to deal with increasing customer objections on pricing.

The point being made was that the customer of a hamburger has absolute right to question the itemized cost of the individual pieces that make up the burger – the buns, the meat, the lettuce, the slice of cheese and so on – to determine the product price. But these items simply add up to make a naked hamburger, not a *McDonald's* one. This was exactly what the salespeople at Apple needed to remember and convey convincingly to their clients. They weren't selling just any old desktop, as, say, IBM was; they were selling an *Apple* product – a product superior in quality and output in every way over its competitors.

Long after that interesting lesson on the naked hamburger, I sat listening to the late management guru C.K. Prahalad speak to a group of Indian CEOs on value-based learning. This was at a time when India's IT industry was at a nascent stage. Prahalad was chiding the CEOs for not pricing their products right. He asked them how much they thought an M.F. Hussain painting costs to make. The price of the canvas, plus the price of a few brushes, paint, an easel may be – they probably cost not more than a few thousand rupees in all. But how much does the painting sell for? Well, a good number of crores for sure. The value of the painting is determined by the perception of the customer. The lesson being driven home was clear: *When you present a product to a customer you tend to think of what it costs to manufacture the product, when you should, instead, be thinking of its perceived value.* Instead of doing cost-plus pricing, Prahalad said, do a minus-pricing from the inherent value of the product.

When you know and believe in the value of your product, you, like McDonald's, are really selling the Golden Arches and not merely two buns with a piece of meat between them. The trick is to believe in the value of the product you're delivering and then persuade the customer to believe in your perception.

■

RAINY DAY, DAMP SPIRIT

There are a million ways to connect with customers. Look for the story behind the product you are selling. Most customers will connect with it instantly and respond to it with the greatest enthusiasm.

I WAS MEETING JOSEPH on a particularly dreary afternoon at the Mindtree office in Redmond, Washington, where he was handling a major customer account. This is basically as far north as it gets for the Pacific North West in the United States. Beyond this lies Canada, where freezing temperatures prevail for the major part of the year. As for Redmond, it sees rain on most days. I don't like the cold too much and avoid the rain if I can. If it was not for a meeting with our customer there, I would not have gone to Redmond at all, despite locals insisting that the three months of summer they get make up for the nine months of rain.

As I shook hands with Joseph, I could see that he wasn't particularly charged up. His weepy mood reflected the incessant rain outside. I asked him what the matter was. He replied, morosely, that all his competitors seemed to have the exact same product he did, and that his customers didn't feel he was offering them anything different at all. (This is a healthy grumpy conversation every salesperson is entitled to have once a quarter with their senior colleagues.)

I grabbed my coat and asked Joseph to do the same. 'We could go someplace and get some coffee. Let's just hang out, shall we?' I said.

We drove a couple of miles north to a strip mall. The place was somewhat deserted at that hour of the day – it was the 'dead time' for this area. The people from downtown had come and gone, having finished their lunch, doggy-bagged the leftovers, picked up their laundry or prescriptions or whatever else they might have needed from the mall, looked at their watches and gone back to their respective cubicles.

At the mall, we stopped at a parking lot next to a deserted bridal store and a photo framer, parked and walked into the Starbucks close by. I chose a cappuccino while Joseph ordered a Columbian coffee, and we settled down at a table on the far side, next to the window.

I had a lot of respect for Joseph, and felt a great deal of sympathy for the slump he was going through. Every salesperson, I knew, needed a sprinkling of 'holy water' from time to time so that they could return to what they do best:

Sell. As a manager, it was my responsibility to administer the occasional sprinkling. The 'holy water' itself had to be different at different times (sometimes coffee and at other times more potent stuff) and with different people, but I have found that it led to cerebral conversations that ended up enriching both the salesperson and I. It was how we bonded, discussed issues, worked the numbers, inspired each other and helped each other succeed.

'Starbucks isn't just coffee,' I found myself saying by way of conversation as we took our first sips. 'People who come to Starbucks usually don't go somewhere else for coffee.'

'Well?' asked Joseph despondently. 'In the United States, you can buy coffee at a gas station, a donut store, a hamburger joint and at a Costa or a Starbucks. Coffee is coffee, isn't it?'

'Have you been to Starbucks's website lately?' I asked, gently leading the conversation toward the point I wanted to make. 'The way they put it, what they sell is more than just coffee.'

'No, I haven't,' replied Joseph. 'What do you mean, more than just coffee?' He took a sip as though to prove his point.

'Okay, let me show you.'

Taking out my cell phone, I opened up the Starbucks website and clicked on the tab titled 'Our Company'. I read out loud to Joseph: *"'Everyday we go to work hoping to do two things: Share great coffee with our friends and help make the world a little better. It was true when the first Starbucks opened in 1971, and it's just as true today...*" Did you notice that they haven't said "our customers"?'

'Yes,' replied Joseph, sitting a little straighter. 'But what do they mean by "making the world a little better"?'

I told him how Starbucks was one of the early supporters of the Rain Forest Alliance and how their efforts in this direction had led to the company becoming a leader in sustainability. They put in a great deal of effort, mostly away from the public eye, in this direction; effort that probably did not have a direct impact on their bottom line. From investing in coffee farmers and their communities, ethical sourcing and the creation of sustainable supply chains, to practising open-source agronomy – theirs was quite the story of a conscionable organization. And the list didn't end there. They were leaders in the emerging segment of 'green retail' as well as in the efforts they made to promote human resources practices that resulted in an internal culture that was all about treating their people with respect and sensitivity.

As I was speaking, Joseph opened the Starbucks site on his phone and was listening to me and browsing at the same time. Suddenly, he looked up, excited.

'Now take a look at this,' he told me, holding up his smartphone like a tablet from Mount Sinai.

The screen read:

EXPECT MORE THAN COFFEE[1]

We're not just passionate purveyors of coffee, but everything else that goes with a full and rewarding coffeehouse experience. We also offer a selection of premium teas, fine pastries and other delectable treats to please the taste buds. And the music you hear in store is chosen for its artistry and appeal.

It's not unusual to see people coming to Starbucks to chat, meet up or even work. We're a neighbourhood gathering place, a part of the daily routine – and we couldn't be happier about it. Get to know us and you'll see: we are so much more than what we brew.

We make sure everything we do is through the lens of humanity – from our commitment to the highest quality coffee in the world, to the way we engage with our customers and communities to do business responsibly.

Thereafter, Joseph's mood picked up considerably. In the remaining fifteen minutes that we were at the coffee shop and later in the car, we spoke of other things. We discussed a proposal that was due the coming Monday; hiring a new sales executive reporting to Joseph for Seattle; his wife's work

---

[1] Taken from Starbucks US's official website, https://www.starbucks.com/about-us/company-information, accessed on 22 May 2017.

at the local community college that she had just joined; and about the upcoming in-company marketing event he was planning. After dropping Joseph back to work, I headed out to the airport, having to budget extra time for the weekend traffic, to top up on fuel, return the rental car I had been driving and then catch a flight back home.

Later that evening, Joseph left me a voicemail. In it he said that when his house was quiet after dinner and he had finished his usual hour of digital detox, it suddenly dawned on him that for the last few months the 'coffee' he had been selling was 'plain' coffee.

Starbucks's messaging had taught him an essential lesson. He realized now that it was Starbucks's story – and not just their coffee – that brought customers back again and again. After all, Starbucks does not sell them knowledge about the process by which coffee is made or how its beans are harvested. It sells them everything else – the story of how Starbucks was established by an English teacher, a history teacher and writer, who started a coffee-roasting business in Seattle; how the intellectual group had an affinity for literary classics like Herman Melville's *Moby Dick*; and how Starbucks got its name. (The story goes that Starbucks very nearly came to be called '*Pequod*', after the whaling ship in *Moby Dick*. But one of the partners didn't like the name and they eventually settled for Starbucks, who was the first mate on the *Pequod*.)

Customers were told how Howard Schultz bought Starbucks, why young people all over the world believe Starbucks is 'green', cool and community-focused, what Starbucks does to train its people, and why and how it helps fund its young workforce to get their college degrees.

Joseph, too, knew that it was time he looked differently at the services he sold. He would possibly go back to the beginning, he said, think about where the founders of Mindtree had come from, the vision they had started the company with and the distance they had traversed from the inception of their dream. He would knit together the story of years of achievement and superior service to ever-expanding markets around the world and the causes the company supported. It made for a good, heartening and inspiring story to go with every product he was meant to sell and he knew it was a sure-shot connect to any customer he approached.

First, though, he would have a cup of Starbucks coffee. For you can buy the coffee anywhere, but where else will you get the story?

■

RAISING THE BAR

Your product must mean the world to you. If you cannot get yourself to be proud of it, do not sell it.

THE SNOW WAS UNRELENTING throughout the drive from Dulles International Airport, Washington DC, to the Marriott Hotel in North Bethesda, Maryland, located in the suburbs of the city. It was past 10 p.m. when I reached the hotel and checked in.

Other than the receptionist, and the barman busy on the far side of the lobby, I spotted no one else. I was tired and hungry which is why, rather than trudge to my room to settle in first, I decided to head to the restaurant adjoining the lobby bar, only to see the chairs overturned on the table and a janitor busy mopping the floor. She looked up from her mop and said in a kind voice, 'We open at six for breakfast.

You can get something to eat at the bar.' I wasn't in the mood for bar food but, left with no choice, thanked her and walked across to where the barman, with no customers to serve, was meticulously wiping the wineglasses, holding each one up against the light to see if there were stains and chips. He saw me coming, greeted me with a cheery 'good evening' as I sat on a barstool and handed me the menu. I knew my choices would be limited but was thankful I would get something to eat.

My spirit soared when I saw something I liked: Shrimp chimichanga with fresh guacamole. I asked for a serving of it, and a glass of Cabernet Sauvignon by the glass to keep me busy until the food arrived. By the time I had finished the wine, the barman arrived with the food and placed it before me. I dug into the chimichanga dipped in guacamole. It was absolutely delightful. I loved it.

The problem with human nature is that when you get something better than what you expected – whatever it may be – you immediately suspect that something is not quite right with the situation.

The menu had said 'freshly made guacamole'. But how, I wondered, could it have been prepared so quickly? And the chimichanga prawns? What about them?

More to get my idle mind to let the issue rest than out of any serious sense of enquiry, I called the barman over. 'Is the chimichanga made fresh here or did you microwave it? Is the guacamole freshly made, as the menu says?' I asked.

He replied, 'Of course, sir. It is all fresh,' and started to walk back to the sink, where he had been cleaning the glasses. Then he paused, turned around and returned to the table.

What followed was a fifteen-minute lecture on the Marriott's values. 'Mr Marriott and his son come here often,' he said, 'and they personally look things over. When there was a blizzard a few years ago, the entire area was without power for days; we brought in the neighbourhood folk, kept them warm and fed them until power was restored. This is the Marriott, sir, and we don't say one thing and do another.'

I realized I had hurt his pride by questioning the quality of the food he had served – the product promise made by the hotel.

When the admonishment was over, I somewhat sheepishly went back to my food. 'Yes, of course,' I said to make up for my blunder, 'it tastes really good. Thank you so much.'

I requested him for a refill of wine, mostly to make amends, and then, to change the topic of conversation, asked him where he was from. It turned out that he was not American. He had been born and brought up in Indonesia and had been working at this hotel for the past year as part of their global rotation programme. The man spoke only manageable

English. He had studied up to high school, trained as a barman in his home country and joined the Marriott.

Long after the meeting with the man who, literally, raised the bar on having pride and love for what his service and product stood for, I fall back on that important lesson: Your product must mean the world to you. If you cannot get yourself to be proud of it, do not sell it. You will be doing a bad job of it, and no favours to yourself.

■

WHO
PAYS
WHOM?

While settling negotiations, do not presume.
Be bold and ask. Clarity often brings with it
relief as well as profit.

D R SRIDHAR MITTA, AN electronics and communications engineer by training, was the first man to be hired by what was known as the Western India Vegetable Products Limited (now known as Wipro Products Limited) when Wipro decided to enter the computer hardware business. At the time, Wipro used to make hydrogenated cooking oil and was in the hydraulics business; this was in 1980. After his PhD at the Oklahoma State University in 1973 – and unlike many of his peers who stayed on in the land of milk and honey – Dr Mitta returned to India to join the Bhabha Atomic Research Centre (BARC) and then the Electronics Corporation of India Ltd (ECI), from where he was head-hunted by Wipro to set up its R&D unit. Over the next three decades or so, Dr Mitta has come to be known as one of the handful of men who raised and then converted a domestic company into a globally respected, multi-billion-dollar giant.

Dr Mitta was my boss for the greater part of my years at Wipro. While he was an R&D man, I came from the world of business. Nonetheless, we shared common ground: our love for business and the professional relationships that spring to life when businesses are set up. I remember wondering more than once where he had gained the rare ability to intertwine his knowledge of technology with a businessman's love for cash, but that was before I learned about his early career.

Dr Mitta hails from Tirupati, a small town in Andhra Pradesh, where his family runs a medicine business. As I understood it, the expectation had been that he would take over the running of the family business and eventually inherit it. However, much to the chagrin of the elders, he left instead to study engineering and then get his master's degree at the Indian Institute of Technology (IIT), Kharagpur. He had made up his mind that he wouldn't be selling medicines in Tirupati.

After IIT came Ohio State University and then his entry into the cyber industries, from where he never looked back. Nonetheless, deep inside him, the small-town business ethos of Tirupati in the 1950s and 1960s had stayed intact. Even as he grew wings, he carried a lot of his beginnings with him; it made him love every bit of the world of global business.

Along the way, he picked up great business perspectives from everyday interactions with everyday folk, no matter where he went in the world. One such incident occurred during his early student days in the United States.

A year after his arrival in the country, as a graduate student at Oklahoma and still unfamiliar with the ways of the locals and their land – their accented English, among other things – Dr Mitta suddenly had to deal with what was a rite of passage for any senior in college in an alien land: Helping a friend (who had just arrived in America) to adjust. This young man was academically brilliant, but he also had a very specific ambition. Having fulfilled his aim of making it to an American university, he developed a strong desire to own a car. The problem was that, as a student from India, he had less than $500 in his pocket. But he was determined to own a vehicle. With that money, he bought the biggest used car he could. It was a huge Plymouth, decades old; it worked, but was a gas-guzzling monster.

Even as Dr Mitta's friend scurried from one campus job to another just to be able to feed the guzzler's insatiable appetite, the boon soon became a bane. It wasn't just the fuel; the car frequently needed oil changes as well. As the days passed, Dr Mitta's friend found his spirits dampened by his expenses on gas, oil and other maintenance issues with his grand car as well as frequent breakdowns. One day, while he and Dr Mitta were riding the sputtering old car on the highway, something gave way. The Plymouth came to a grinding halt and refused to move despite their best attempts to revive it.

By now, the owner himself had become a total wreck. He had no money left for yet another round of repairs. As the two young men sat contemplating fate, fate itself showed up (as it does ever so often) in the form of a police patrol car. The policeman knew from one quick look that the stalled car would have to be towed to the nearest junkyard. He radioed for a towing agency. In no time, a tow truck appeared with a large man at the wheel. Very few words were exchanged, and most of them between the tow-truck driver and the cop.

The decision was made. The tow-truck driver nodded his head, asked the two men to get inside the old junk, attached the stalled car by a chain to the tow truck's rear and made for the car graveyard. Neither Dr Mitta nor his companion spoke a word, both silently dreading the financial consequences that were now looming large. Who was going to pay the towing charges?

At the junkyard, the burly tow-trucker jumped out of his vehicle with a pad and a pen in hand. Dr Mitta and his crestfallen friend watched him with sinking hearts. The man gave the old Plymouth a last assessing look and started scribbling some numbers while muttering to himself. When the man was done with what seemed like an estimate for repairs, he looked up from the pad and declared in a voice of finality, 'That will be $250.'

Dr Mitta's friend nearly collapsed. He had nowhere to turn. Where on earth was he going to arrange the money from? At this moment, just as his friend was going to offer his services to the junkyard man to be able to square up, Dr Mitta had a brainwave.

'Wait a minute,' he countered in a voice of assumed confidence. 'Who pays whom?'

The tow-truck guy looked nonplussed for a moment and replied, 'I pay you, of course.'

Dr Mitta's friend simply could not believe his ears. Slowly, reality dawned. The driver had been estimating the junk value of the car and calculating his towing charges, and now he was making an offer to the duo to buy their wreck!

Dr Mitta and his friend returned with real cash in their pocket and a few lessons never to be forgotten: While making a deal, never lose hope. In a difficult business situation, all too often, we arrive at conclusions in our own heads and make presumptions about a situation that may not be the reality. It always helps to play on your chances. Be bold and ask. Clarity often brings with it relief as well as profit.

■

THEORY E

People who sell must be supremely comfortable with the act of asking. The point is to never fear rejection and to not give up on a chance by giving in to that fear.

THERE IS A STORY that goes something like this.

A long time ago, somewhere in an ancient Indian kingdom, there was a river that flowed past a city. As was the prevailing custom in those days, the people from the so-called 'higher' castes always bathed upstream, while their 'lesser' brethren would perform their ablutions further downstream.

One day, while a man from a 'higher' caste was bathing, another fellow appeared to take a dip some distance downstream, given his station. While the two were going about their job, a third man arrived with an adult elephant to give the pachyderm a bath and chose an appropriate spot nearby. The elephant bathed with great joy, trumpeting and frolicking, the mahout scrubbing him dutifully. It was quite the spectacle and, enthralled by the sight, the two bathers forgot about their purpose and watched.

After some time, the man bathing upstream asked the mahout, 'Brother, will you give me your elephant?'

The mahout, now perched on top of the animal's head, scrubbing away, laughed good-naturedly and went about his work without saying a word.

The two onlookers watched the process for a little while longer. Then the same man cleared his throat and again asked, 'O brother, can I have your elephant please?'

This time, the mahout gave him a scornful look before going back to his work. He said nothing.

More time passed.

Now, apparently oblivious to his earlier failed attempts, the man bathing upstream moved closer to the elephant and repeated his request.

This time, the mahout was visibly disgusted and, guiding the elephant out of the water, rode away.

The bather downstream was perplexed with what he had just witnessed. Unable to contain himself, he now, most respectfully, asked the other man, 'Oh wise one, didn't you know that the man would never give you the elephant? You just kept asking for it...'

To this, the first man retorted, 'That may be true, but

do you think he would have ever thought of giving me the elephant had I not asked in the first place?'

People who sell must be supremely comfortable with the act of asking. You have to ask for things all the time. Ask for direction, ask for leads, ask for referrals, ask for inside information, ask for a request for proposal, ask for the order and, above all, ask for the money. There may be rejections; there may be objections; there may be detractors; there may be obstacles of many kinds. The point is to never fear rejection and to not give up on a chance by giving in to that fear.

Ask. You have nothing to lose.

■

SHAKING YOUR ASH

How frequently does a 'welcome' sign await a salesperson? In reality, not so often. In such circumstances persistence will inevitably pay.

I N APRIL 2010, WHILE returning from a trip abroad, my wife Susmita and I landed at the Frankfurt airport on time, all set to board our connecting flight to Bengaluru. My co-founder Janakiraman Srinivasan's daughter, Anita, was getting married. We had planned for months in advance to be with them for the event.

On our arrival at the Frankfurt airport, however, we were told there was a volcano in Iceland that had decided it was time to spit out ash. The ash particles were spreading all over Europe from Iceland, and that had made flying in European airspace a hazardous business. Airport after airport was closing down, and we had been told that no flights would take off from Frankfurt for God-alone-knew-how-long. We were well and truly stuck.

After ten hours of free tea, coffee and sandwiches at the lounge, and many trips in between to the exasperated airline representative – not to mention endlessly logging in to CNN. com and other news portals for updates – I realized that we would have to stay at the airport overnight. By every indication, even speculating on when flights would be allowed to take off was futile. By then the airport wore the look of a refugee camp with thousands of stranded passengers camped on every bit of free space. On seeing this we began to consider getting out of the airport to find a hotel to at least get a good night's sleep.

With that thought in mind, I went to the immigration counter. I had a valid German visa, but the policeman at the counter told me to stay back at the airport because Susmita's German visa had expired just a week ago. It was terribly frustrating, but an expired visa was an expired visa.

When we returned to the lounge, the person in charge there had more bad news. The lounge was going to close down at 10 p.m., and we would have to leave. This meant spending the night sitting on a chair outside the gates, or sleeping on the carpet somewhere. A few hundred camp cots had been spread out in the corridors, one next to another; but the thought of sleeping in a crowded space after the exhausting wait was not a particularly comforting one.

Attending the wedding was by now out of the question.

The issue was how to survive the discomfort of being held captive without a change of clothes, not knowing if this would be a one-, two- or three-day ordeal.

In times like these, you often end up making friends with strangers. People reach out to each other and, based on a test of familiarity, they bond and make small teams that then look for ways out of their shared misery. In the lounge, there were three other Indians, who were as we discovered over a conversation much younger, but in the same boat as us. They, too, had tried to get past German immigration – they had pleaded for a day's visa, tried to tell the unrelenting authorities that all they wanted was to spend the night in a hotel somewhere, even going on to prove that they had the money to do so. But to no avail. They had been stonewalled, just as we had been.

Left with no choice, we set off together in search of a quiet corner, and somehow managed to get through the night.

The next morning, we returned to the lounge as soon as it opened. As the day progressed – between the anxious in and out of the lounge for some news of the airport resuming operations – we heard from someone that German immigration had relented and were letting some passengers out. We scampered en masse to the immigration windows to try our luck, only to be told that we either had to be older than seventy or younger than three to be allowed to leave.

Susmita and I gave up; we returned to where we were before and slumped back in our chairs.

A couple of hours went by. The others in our group had wandered off somewhere, but soon one of them returned, and coming to my side surreptitiously whispered, 'Go to Terminal A. There is an empty booth with a bearded cop. If you are Indian, he is giving you a day visa.'

That didn't make any sense, I told him. Germans are strict followers of rules; a 'no' from them is a 'no'.

'Yes, yes,' our newly made friend insisted, showing me his passport. 'See, I got mine; now you must rush before the man goes away.'

We ran like we never had before.

At Terminal A, there was no queue; a lone policeman sat at the immigration counter. He looked at us and, without a word, opened our passports and stamped our visas. We escaped to a hotel as quickly as we could.

Our benefactor – who, like us, had been stonewalled in Terminal B but had then, while we sat around moaning, gone to Terminal A and found a completely unexpected solution to the problem – was, of course, a salesman by profession. Salesmen, it seems, have an amulet that reminds them that 'no' does not mean 'never'. It could mean 'not now'; in this case, it appeared to be a variant: 'Not here.'

In selling, 'no' does not mean the end of the line. It simply means working on a refusal or an objection and finding a different approach; it's all in a day's work. The salesman at the counter in a sari shop or at an electronics showroom deals with rejection everyday, as does the seller in what we call the business-to-business world, where you may be selling anything from expensive medical equipment to oilfield drilling services. Resilience and persistence are a salesperson's talismans.

Whenever I think of the subject of rejection, I wonder how frequently a welcome sign awaits a salesperson. In reality, not so often. Instead, salespeople mostly get to hear one of the following statements, a variant of the same or some other more imaginative door-closer:

> 'We are not looking for a vendor at this time.'
>
> 'You need to be assessed at Software Engineering Institute (SEI) Level 5 before we talk to you.'
>
> 'You have never worked in our domain.'
>
> 'You do not know our technology.'
>
> 'You are not on our approved vendor list.'
>
> 'We are reducing our list of vendors.'

What a good salesperson needs to remember is where there is a gate, there will be a gatekeeper, and even if you can't get your way around them, there are always other gates in other terminals. You've just got to be persistent and find them.

■

A MEETING
WITH
ST PAUL

Today, marketing is shifting from the war room to the battlefield. Once the key prospects have been identified, it becomes all about using laser-guided strikes to communicate a customized story.

NOT SO FAR BACK, towards the end of 2016, after a series of intense engagements at Mindtree Kalinga's Global Learning Centre in Bhubaneswar, I decided to take a vacation and spend some time alone. A bureaucrat friend of mine, Pradeep Jena, suggested I vacation on a small island he knew of, in the middle of Lake Chilika. The island, named Rajhans, had a small rest house maintained by the Forest Department. 'It's the perfect place for your writing work,' Pradeep said. 'It's very quiet, with no tourists and no crowds.' And so, taking his advice, I made my way there.

Upon my arrival at Rajhans, just as I was getting off the boat, I realized that solitude wasn't exactly what I was fated for. The caretaker, who had come to receive me at the small jetty, proudly told me that there was already an 'American sahib' staying at the rest house. I wasn't too pleased, but there was little I could do about it.

As I walked up to the rest house, which stood a little away from the lakeshore and was cosily shielded by tall trees, I saw a thinly built man lounging in the veranda in front of the bungalow. He looked like the kind of person who has careful eating habits and exercises routinely; I surmised that he was probably in his late forties.

Seeing me, he stood up and offered his hand. 'Welcome to Rajhans,' he said. 'I am Paul, Paul Gottsegen.'

'Subroto, Subroto Bagchi,' I heard myself saying. I wasn't sure I wanted to have a conversation.

'Welcome to heaven,' he declared with friendly authority. 'I come here once every few years, all the way from the cold east coast of the United States. Is it your first time here?'

'Yes, indeed,' I replied. 'I will see you later, though.' I gestured at the small suitcase and computer bag that I had to lug to the room allotted to me.

'Sure,' he said. 'You want help with that luggage?'

'No, I've got it,' I assured him. 'I'm good.'

He waved at me and went back to his seat, basking in the winter sun that filtered through the thin casuarina leaves. I went to my room, dumped my stuff and decided it was time for some tea and writing before lunch.

Paul and I met again when the caretaker brought lunch for us, a lovely local fare of fish, shrimp and crabs. Paul ate like a local too, astonishing me with the dexterity of his fingers. As we chatted over the meal, he revealed that he was a marketing guy.

'Marketing, not sales,' he emphasized.

'Yes, yes, I know.'

'I don't find many Indians who know the distinction. What do you do?'

'I'm writing a book on selling,' I replied.

'No kidding!' He looked up from the crab he was shelling and announced, 'We've got to talk.'

After a fabulous meal, Paul and I decided to take a boat ride to the confluence of the lake and the sea, where Chilika embraced the Bay of Bengal. We saw a few dolphins on the way and lingered on the water until sunset. Then, carefully avoiding the many shrimp nets and sailing past cynical-looking cormorants perched on the bamboo poles rising from the waterbed, we returned to the rest house.

It had been a good day, and as we sat down in the veranda, some hot tea arrived and we got talking.

Paul had studied at the Wharton School at the University of Pennsylvania, Philadelphia, he said, and since graduation had worked in many large companies in various roles. He had worked his way to the top, and could now afford to take a week off every year to return to Chilika like the thousands of migratory birds that came there all the way from Siberia, Tibet and other northern regions.

Taking a sip of tea, Paul told me an interesting story.

'My dad, Arthur Gottsegen,' he said, 'was a great salesman. A really nice guy, well-liked too. Our family business was to do with plastics – household items like garbage cans, dishpans, toothbrushes – anything that was made from injection-moulded plastic. I have fond memories of seeing him in action and when you told me about your book it sparked many long-lost memories.'

'Anything in particular?' I asked.

'Well, yeah,' he nodded. 'One cool story is from when we were in New Orleans. The region he covered when he was in his twenties included Arkansas. He used to call on this guy named Sam who had a small retail business. Sam liked my dad a lot; my dad said that in a business like that of plastics, a lot of people just buy from the salesperson they personally like. Sam took a strong liking to my father and as his business took off, with more stores being opened, Sam became a big client of my dad's company. That was Sam Walton, the founder of Walmart.'

Wow, I thought. *What a story*. I was glad now that I had met Paul and decided to make the most of my time with him. The story about Sam was a good segue into the conversation that ensued as some more tea arrived. I asked Paul: Having watched his father at work and from being in marketing himself, what was the one seminal advice he had for salespeople?

'Anyone in sales,' he said, 'or, for that matter, anyone who has a client-facing job with a revenue target, must use their marketing departments to greater advantage. Most do not do that.'

'How is that? Please tell me more.'

'Salespeople often do not know how to use marketing tools to train themselves. And, mind you, one-time training does not really help.'

'Train in what?' I asked, a little confused by his words.

'Training to build the robustness of an attack and defence strategy,' he replied firmly. 'Also, training to develop two or three sales hooks – things that make your message to customers both easy and differentiated.'

'Hmm,' I replied. 'Easy and differentiated... That is interesting.'

'Well, easy–firstly, so that the salespeople are able to deliver the message about the product most effectively and, secondly, so that the clients, the customers, get it. No one has the time for complex, sophisticated stuff, you know. And differentiated – so that, with a quick instance, the customer knows how you are different from the competition, what makes you special.'

'There are tools for that kind of thing…' I remarked.

'Yes, that is right,' he agreed. 'An offshoot of the marketing-assisted training process is to create what is called the playbook. The basic idea of a playbook comes from the world of sports, you know. You go to every play with five offensive and three defensive plays. And you train your mind in these over and over again before every game.'

'How so? Give me an example of the five offensive plays,' I asked.

'Okay,' he said. 'Try thinking of selling the same product using five different ideas:

- ✓ My product is value for money.
- ✓ My product is designed for your current, specific need to balance rapid deployment with cash flow.
- ✓ My product comes with a use-now-and-pay-later scheme.
- ✓ My product has the best fuel efficiency that fits exactly into your corporate sustainability programme to consciously reduce the carbon footprint of the production floor.
- ✓ We can get my product installed rapidly because we can move it from our warehouse right next door.

Basically, you should never go to play with a single pitch, a single story.'

'And what about the three defences?' I asked.

'You have to anticipate the objections,' he said. 'For example, the client could tell you that you may be offering value for money but the maintenance fees that kick in after a year are way too high. Or that your product may be good for today but is not expandable to meet their future growth. Or even that for the fuel efficiency you promise, you are way too expensive compared to your nearest competition and you're making the total cost of ownership much higher.'

'A playbook, I get it now…like in a war game, a simulation,' I said, musing over what he had told me.

'Yes,' he nodded. 'And that leads me to another thing – the idea of embedded marketing.'

I frowned at that, curious.

'Marketing is shifting from the war room to the battlefield,' he said. 'There was a time when marketing was about carpet-bombing a whole set of prospects with all kinds of messages, hoping something would stick in someone's mind, and that they would then invite you in for a conversation. Today, it is about zeroing in on key prospects and using laser-guided strikes to communicate a customized story.'

He looked at me to check if I was following; satisfied that he had a good student, he continued. 'This shift in approach requires continuous conversation between the salespeople and their marketing colleagues,' he said. 'And do you know something interesting? The marketing–sales tango is increasingly getting even more fine-tuned for deal-based marketing. Wherever large deals are involved, marketing is brought in, side by side with sales, to make it happen. Like creating a microsite for one prospect alone, or making customized T-shirts with the client's house colours on them for all the team members going in for a negotiation, or designing customer-specific collaterals for a customer visit. It is all about paying attention to the smallest detail and making the buyer feel that they are always on your mind. You know the story about the brown M&Ms, right?'

'No, I don't,' I confessed.

'There was a very famous rock band in the late 1970s and early 1980s called Van Halen. They put on one of the largest – if not *the* largest – live show productions at that time. For their big production to work, especially in older venues or in smaller cities that didn't have the infrastructure they required, there were many preparations that the local venues needed to make to handle electricity, the weight of all the equipment and so on. These preparations were included by Van Halen in their contract, and as a test to see how thoroughly the local production team read the requirements the band randomly inserted a sentence right in the middle to the effect of, "There will be no brown M&Ms in the backstage area, or the promoter will forfeit the entire contract." Obviously, brown M&Ms taste just the same as the others, but this was Van Halen's brilliant method of testing the commitment of the organizers. If they saw brown M&Ms in the jar in their dressing room, they would know they needed to inspect everything extra carefully because the local production venue had not paid attention to detail.'

'Ah, what a great story!' I exclaimed.

'Yes, it is. The importance of paying attention to the fine print cannot be underplayed. And, by the way,' he grinned, 'have you heard of something called a "social selling index"?'

'What is that?' I asked.

'Well, selling is all about numbers, right? As in, what is the value of the business you are chasing, how many deals are you closing, how much of your target are you meeting, how much your commission is, and that kind of stuff. Salespeople understand all this. But what about using numbers to find out your social selling index?'

'Do you mean measuring social selling skills like using Internet-based tools that connect you to a wide circle of people?' I asked.

'Yes. A salesperson who uses LinkedIn, for example, can know his social selling skills as a number. He can monitor that on a regular basis, and compare it to the numbers other salespeople are putting up. It is simply not enough to know the number. Rather, it is important to keep improving on it. Marketing can help you get there.'

'And how is that?'

'Everyone has an online presence,' he said. 'Beyond just the online presence – the presentation layer of who you are – you have to engage and you have to measure yourself on how well you are engaging. And that is entirely about creating content. Today's selling is largely about content. Content is the new weapon.

'While LinkedIn is the new calling card for today's salespeople, what you do with it will take you from the also-online ones to the great ones. You've got to know how to be more presentable in the online world. Your marketing team can help you there. You may have heard this before, but thanks to the World Wide Web your customer is researching you – sometimes well before you have started your own research. In that sense, you are in your customer's presence long before you physically arrive there. You deliver the calling card long before you show up in person.'

Paul paused after that long discourse and, just then, the caretaker arrived to tell us that dinner had been served.

We stood up.

In a moment of brief silence, I became aware of the whispering winds speaking to the casuarina leaves, the sea waves breaking on a deserted beach not far from where we were, and a lone owl hooting from somewhere afar.

My mind wandered to the time when I was a cub and 'marketing' was all about a bunch of people in the company's headquarters who spent hours in meetings with advertising agencies and had little to do with the salespeople selling the product on the ground. So much has changed for the better, I mused. The two-pronged fork of sales and marketing could prove to be the strongest tool to hook the customer.

■

THE POWER OF THE POINT

Forcing the client to follow your thought process rather than speaking in alignment with theirs doesn't send out a good message.

THE LIGHTS WERE OUT in most parts of the building.

I had buried myself so deep in a draft report to my board that I had completely lost track of time. It was only when I became aware of the soft hum of the air conditioner that I realized I was alone. It must have been a couple of hours since my administrative aide had left for the evening; I had wished her goodnight absent-mindedly, somewhat in a state of stupor.

I leaned back in my chair, tired, and closed my eyes. The report I was to present was a routine matter, but for some days now I had been thinking about how I would present it and presentations of this kind in general. It was possibly a conversation that I had recently had with Neo Mehra, a long-time associate, that had set off such thoughts in my mind; of late, I found myself going over the lessons I had picked up over a career of making presentations.

Leaning back further in my chair to stretch my back and legs, I soon fell asleep.

'Every time I sit through people's presentations I wonder why they don't get the basics right.' It was Neo Mehra. He was clearly disgruntled.

'What?' I was startled for a moment. *Where had he come from?* The next instant, I found myself asking, 'What do you mean?'

'Salespeople,' Neo grumbled. 'Almost all of them; they tend to push content about themselves. Why don't they begin with the client? Why don't they personalize and contextualize the slide deck and say: "This is what we have learnt about you, your needs, and this is why we would like to share the following information with you"?'

I nodded. It is something that bothered me as well; badly contextualized information is almost as bad as no information at all. Forcing the client to follow *your* thought process rather than speaking in alignment with *theirs* doesn't send out a good message. In most presentations, though, the voice is me, me, me.

'Wait a minute,' I replied, leaping into the conversation. 'Why not begin even before that? Even before they make the pitch and begin to talk about their ideas, solutions, whatever, wouldn't it be a good idea to identify a coach in the client organization? The smart thing would be to send the coach a draft presentation and get them to go over it in advance. The coach would be able to offer guidance and, in either case, will appreciate the diligence.'

'The best salespeople do that,' Neo nodded in agreement. 'But I see them do something else very well too. They often say, "I have a lot of slides but I will walk you through the important ones, and would be happy to dive into specifics when you want. And, in any case, I will be leaving the full deck behind so you can go through it at leisure."

'During my time,' he picked up a moment later, 'I have seen a couple of really good salespeople. They send their presentations in ahead of time; they use their meetings to sit around the table and have a conversation, using the deck simply as a guide. This is a good use of time; people can be engaged, you can have eye contact and you come across as consultative.'

'I have seen a few really bad sales presentations as well,' I remarked, mulling over some of the not-so-effective presentations that I had sat through. 'Tell me, what drives you nuts about bad presentations?'

That really opened the floodgates.

'They don't arrive before time,' Neo began somewhat

heatedly. 'The number of times I've had to remind my juniors to arrive early, to check where the light switches are, where the blind controls are, who should be seated where... Sometimes, they don't even pre-test the video they are going to play!'

'Bad planning,' I remarked, nodding in agreement. 'Much better to arrive early and invest some time in preparing for the presentation than to have your presentation fail halfway because you didn't check everything in advance.'

Neo was not done. 'They don't spell-check their slides either,' he continued, waving his arms in frustration. 'They think nothing of using logos and charts and graphs downloaded from the Internet without permission or acknowledgment of the source. Do you know how unprofessional that comes across as? No one wants to work with someone who doesn't do their homework; or, worse, steals it from the Internet!'

I opened my mouth to agree but Neo was on a roll now, his words spewing out faster and faster in agitation. 'And their presentation skills! Abysmal! They don't make eye contact with everyone,' he rumbled disapprovingly. 'They keep their gaze fixed on one or two people in the room. They don't check for comprehension, they don't ask if their audience is following them. They don't pay extra attention to those who have joined in on video or on the phone. They don't carry a hard copy of their presentation as a backup, just in case...'

'You certainly didn't have to think long about that one,'

I muttered in response. I could have added my own gripes, of which the top slot would go to ignoring remote people on an audio or video bridge. People get engrossed with those in the room and completely forget those who may be attending virtually.

It was time to change tack. I asked Neo, 'What constitutes the flip side, though? What makes for a good presentation? What can someone do to make sure a pitch goes well?'

'Well,' said Neo, 'preparation is always the key. In my experience, good salespeople rehearse their presentations and seek feedback from their friends at work, even if it is the 400th time that they are making the same pitch. It's the audience, you see; for the audience, it's always the first time.'

'Preparation and rehearsal,' I muttered, nodding in agreement. 'What else?'

'There are a lot of little things to keep in mind,' Neo replied authoritatively. 'For example, good salespeople always check how much time they have for their presentation after their audience has arrived and everyone has settled down. They may have been assigned a certain amount of time beforehand, but things may have changed; these people are thoughtful, and they show they can make adjustments. As they speak, the emphasis is on informing and not impressing. That makes them come across as trusted advisors and not someone who is just there to sell. They tell their audience upfront whether they like to take questions as they go along, or if they'd prefer questions to be held until the end of the presentation.'

'Right,' I nodded again. 'All of that does a lot to break the ice and set up a fruitful meeting. But what else can one do?'

'Well,' Neo said thoughtfully, 'in putting together their presentation, even when it comes to what slides to show, good salespeople focus on the information that their audience needs, and what the audience's mood and time requirements will allow for. Good presenters make sure to cover only the relevant slides; they don't seek to push it all down their audience's throat. And there's more. Good presenters pause often, and look around to see if everyone's following their presentation. They listen deeply before starting to answer questions. They reply in short sentences. They admit if they don't know something, write it down and promise to revert. They keep ample time for Q and A, seek feedback at the end and get closure on the next steps. They thank the client the same day with a follow-up list.'

'That's a tall order,' I remarked with a frown. 'Especially for someone just starting out.'

'It will only be a tall order if they are not using their firm's resources well,' Neo replied firmly.

'What do you mean?' I asked. 'What resources?'

'Well,' he replied, 'they could, for example, learn to make use of their firm's marketing department intelligently.

Bringing them in on the deal early on, making each pitch unique and personalized... And then there's the legal angle they have to think of as well...'

'Hold on a minute,' I began...but just then there was a loud bang.

I jumped up with a start, only to find that I was alone; Neo had disappeared, and in his place stood the cleaner, looking apologetic, picking up the mop from the floor.

'Sorry, sir,' the man muttered in embarrassment as I wiped the sleep from my eyes and yawned and stretched mightily. 'I thought everyone had left for the night. I can come back later to clean your office.'

'Take your time,' I replied, grabbing my coat from the back of my chair and chuckling as I thought of the dream I'd just had. 'I was just leaving... But tell me, is anyone from our marketing department still in office?'

■

THE LEGAL EAGLE

Hooking a customer with attractive pitches is the rule, but commitments to clients should be made with caution and with complete attention to the legal consequences of such promises.

A FEW WEEKS AFTER my trip to Chilika, I met a friend, Erwan Carpentier, over dinner.

Erwan has made a career of advising big companies on international laws that govern contracts. A slender, boyishly handsome, soft-spoken man, Erwan hardly comes across as a legal eagle. The first time we met, I remember asking him about his French origins.

'I'm not originally from France,' he had replied. 'I'm from a place called Corsica. Do you know of it?'

'Yes, of course. But after Napoleon Bonaparte,' I told him, 'you are really the second Corsican I know.'

He was mighty pleased that I knew about his island, and with that we became friends.

In the evening when I met him, he looked a little preoccupied. I asked him what the matter was, and he unburdened his worries.

His story went something like this.

Erwan's company had a long-standing business relationship with an American client. They did more than $20 million worth of business in a year with that client alone. A few weeks ago, Erwan told me, the client had awarded them a new multi-year, multi-million-dollar contract, but a week later their sales guy had been summoned and informed that the order had been cancelled.

'Why did they do that?' I asked. 'What had changed suddenly?'

'Well, the client found two problems in the proposal,' he replied. 'Whoever wrote the proposal had done a cut-and-paste job from a website that didn't belong to them, and in another part of the proposal, the individual had reproduced a couple of paragraphs from a white paper someone else had written and had failed to acknowledge the source.'

'Isn't that kind of stuff avoidable? Isn't there a simple thumb rule to follow?' I asked.

'Sometimes people don't understand the details,' he said. 'A lot of things we do for clients is "work for hire". That means that the Intellectual Property (IP) rights on the work belong to the client. You can't sell it again, even if you created it ir the first place. Again, you may have created it but you were, under the law, hired, commissioned and paid to create it for the client who paid you and it is he who now owns it. Think of an advertising campaign an agency creates for a client. It belongs to the client now. They can't be lifting parts of it to propose to another client.'

I nodded sympathetically.

'Then, of course, is the knowledge that we acquire as we work with and for customers. There is generic knowledge about the customer and the customer's industry, and then there is specific knowledge about the client, their plans, processes, practices and a whole bunch of things. When I sell to a new client or move from this client to another for a new project, I can only take the generic knowledge and nothing more. I cannot take and reuse anything that is client-specific.'

'Tell me more,' I suggested. 'What other legal bloopers do salespeople need to look out for while making a presentation or a pitch?'

'Salespeople are masters of cut-and-paste,' shrugged Erwan. 'They often use clients' names, logos, lists of customers and even talk about how the client uses its tools and processes in business. You cannot do that without taking express permission. You cannot cut and paste any stuff from the client's website. It is there for anyone to read, yes, but that's it. You can read it, yes, but you can't reproduce it. Most salespeople are not aware that just because something pops up when you search for it on Google it does not mean you can use the information for your own purpose. Just because a picture, chart or piece of data shows up on your search doesn't mean that you can download it and use it. Whenever you refer to something in a proposal, like data, opinions, points of view or whatever, which you actually learnt from somewhere else, you are obligated to acknowledge its source. Here's an example: Sometimes salespeople attend seminars and conferences. They hear someone deliver a talk and carry home the hard copy of the presentation given away to the attendees. Often, they tend to reproduce someone else's slides or material from someone else's presentation in their next proposal. Salespeople love to quote trends and market shares and stuff; and some of them are of the opinion: "What a joy it is that a Gartner, a Forrester, an IDG has done all the work for me and all I need to do is cut and paste it and use it in my presentation!"'

'Yes, I too have seen quite a bit of this. And what about making overeager statements in order to win business?' I asked Erwan. 'Doesn't it create a weak foundation? It's like saying, "My services are the best in the industry and I warrant that I will deliver on time," even though that may not be true or you know the delivery will not, or cannot, come about?'

'Yes, indeed,' he nodded. 'Many a time I find salespeople making such confident, overreaching statements in proposals, and in the emails they send to customers and prospects. Hooking a customer with attractive pitches is the rule. Every company puts their best foot forward during the pre-sale discussion or as a response to a request for proposal; but there's a catch. They forget that any representation or warranty at the pre-contractual stage can lead to severe damages in courts of law around the world. You know how the IT services provider Hewlett-Packard (HP)/Electronic Data Systems (EDS) in the United Kingdom had to pay the BSkyB group a huge sum – £200 million – as an interim payment for fraudulent and negligent misrepresentation, isn't it?'

I almost fell off my chair at what Erwan had just said. I had heard about the HP case but had not quite registered the fallout and the size of the damage.

'Well,' he continued, 'it could have been worse. BSkyB originally sought damages of something like £700 million! That is why I tell my salespeople, continue to present your best side during pre-sales pitches but never exaggerate your capacities or oversell yourself in areas where you do not control everything or ones that don't exist.'

'Pitch hard, but pitch carefully,' I smiled. 'Would you agree?'

'Yes,' he said morosely. 'If only our own fellow had kept that in mind.'

While returning home after my dinner with Erwan, I thought about how complex business transactions had become. The entire fortune of a company can get destroyed if we don't pay attention to the legal consequences of our actions. Everyone in an organization, from the CEO to the junior-most executive, must know the basics of the laws that govern a business. With the rise of cross-border transactions, the imperative is even larger.

The best insurance against such an outcome is to take the counsel of an Erwan Carpentier, not after but before you sign a deal so that, unlike Napoleon the Corsican, you don't have to face your Waterloo.

■

NO GREEK,
NO LATIN

Unlike the more forceful act of convincing, the end goal of persuasion is not winning, the agenda is not conquest. That is why persuasion is the higher power.

Back in 2001, our younger daughter, Niti, was blossoming into her teenage angst years, complete with suspicion towards governments and big businesses. She had moved to a vegan diet, given up leather shoes and belts and bags and then, to my utter consternation, announced one day that she had decided to take up Latin as an elective in high school.

I could clearly see that I was losing the battle against my children going astray and thought it my solemn duty to save her from herself, one last time. I decided to sit her down for a father–daughter talk, basically to wean her away from the clutches of what I believed were weird ideas that would hurt her chances of securing a medical, engineering or law school and of having what I then perceived to be a 'real' career.

There was just one thought raging in my mind: *I don't want my daughter to become a hippie!*

The conversation with Niti didn't last long. She had her antennae of suspicion and angst up, even as we settled down to talk. I too had made up my mind to be bold and began by asking her why she wanted to study a dead language.

'Did you say *dead*?' She sounded like a volcano about to erupt. I cringed.

'Who reads Latin these days and in what way will it help you in college?' I asked as gently as I could, trying to sound wise and invested. But to her I came across as being critical.

'Dad, all that doesn't matter to me,' she said dramatically. 'And do you know why Latin is a dead language?'

I didn't reply. I knew it was a bait.

She was indignant. 'Because people like you don't care about it, and that is why it's all the more important for me to save the language.'

Having declared her victory, she picked up her coffee and walked away. More than a decade later, she is a Latin scholar and teaches the language to high-school children.

I, too, began to take an interest in the language as she learnt more of it and, over time, came to understand some of the key aspects of studying the classics and classical languages. Even though I have not come anywhere close to where she is in her pursuit today, I began to appreciate the origin of word

This, too, happened over a father–daughter talk with Niti, though nowhere as disastrous as the earlier one. We were reminiscing, in fact, about the previous incident, which had made her choice of subject for higher studies final.

What I should have done, Niti said, was to *persuade* her instead of trying to *convince* her, though I had not done the latter well either, she remarked with a chuckle. 'You should have known the difference between the two, Dad. You pride yourself on your selling abilities after all,' she said.

A sobering thought. I asked her to explain to me the difference between the two words.

'The word "persuade",' she gently told me, 'originated in the late fifteenth century from a combination of the Latin *"per"*, which meant "through, to completion" and *"suadere"* which meant "advise". The word "convince", on the other hand, actually means to "overcome or defeat in argument", derived from the Latin *convincere*, combining "con", a prefix denoting "with", and *"vincere"* meaning "conquer". The former is about staying the course, persisting with an advisory approach. It is about offering expertise and consultation, and helping people with your wisdom. Unlike the more forceful act of convincing, the end goal here is not winning, the agenda is not conquest. That is why persuasion is the higher power.'

My daughter was absolutely spot-on. As someone who prides himself on his ability to sell, I had missed making use of finer points of persuasion when it came to discussing her future. Perhaps many salespeople overlook exactly this when they approach a prospect and reach a certain stage of negotiation.

So, what are these finer points?

Persuasion begins with sensing.

You engage with all five sensory organs and gauge the other person. What is she feeling right now? What is going on in her mind? What could she be looking for? What may be of concern and consequence for her right now? This is fundamentally different from being aware singlemindedly of what you are looking for, and what is of concern and consequence for you. The one consideration in your mind should be: is what you are offering in alignment with your customer's needs?

Persuasion requires us to respect the other person.

The customer must be handled with great respect, whoever he or she may be (in my case, it was my daughter, a student in high school). Political leaders get that one thing right. They don't dumb down their pitch; they don't ever think of the most illiterate voter as ignorant. They are never patronizin or condescending. Their message to their constituency is that of respect and understanding.

Persuasion requires suspending judgement.

Saying that Latin is a dead language did not help my cause. It never would have, because I was conveying how fixed I am in my notions and also that I had not thought about the issue from all possible angles. Salespeople must continuously use their observation and judgement while dealing with prospects and customers to constantly stay on their toes and be effective sellers. But judgement is one thing and being judgemental is something quite different. If the other side thinks you are judgemental, they will likely walk out of the conversation, much like my daughter, even if there existed a possibility of negotiation and persuasion.

Persuasion requires enquiry.

We need to be able to ask questions before, during and after meeting the customer. What has brought the customer this far? Who does the customer compare him/herself with? What is the definition of success for the customer? Why is the customer fascinated with certain things and wary of others? Constantly asking questions makes for clarity and transparency regarding where the product may fit into the customer's scheme of things.

Asking questions requires deep, reflective listening, and a clear mindspace. The more you listen, the greater will be your power to persuade. People end up listening to what you have to say once they see that you are listening to them. After all, it is true that we like those who listen when we speak. It means they care.

Persuasion begins with recognizing the emotional needs of people and pitching to their emotions.

You cannot appeal to people's emotions simply by quoting facts and data. Whether it is a politician selling the idea of change to a community or a nation, or a high-end car salesman selling a dream to a guy suffering from a mid-life crisis, the point is to appeal to people's emotive needs. Only when the mind is open, empathetic and intuitive can the data do its bit.

Persuasion requires advisory ability.

Advisory ability comes from personal knowledge and experience. A key aspect of knowledge and experience is the ability to offer references and bring to bear the power of one's own network for the benefit of the customer. I may not know how a windfarm works but if you as my customer want to visit a windfarm I can take you to one and I know people there who would generously host your visit. Building variou networks outside of your work-related sphere helps to widen your horizon. The combination of knowledge and experience that this brings will enable you to curate different options and choices for the customer. In persuasive selling, the seller is able to present many options and explain the outcome of each one of the choices. On the other hand, if you set out to convince your customer, the field narrows down to just one intended outcome – you can have any colour you like, as long as it is black.

Of course, persuasion should not be about meaningless persistence. There are times when persuasion does not work. In moments like that, one has to suspend the act. Allow for mental and physical space. Change the subject. Take a walk. Return to the table with an open mind and a fresh perspective.

Throughout the process – and, yes, it is a process – you must be respectful of even the smallest concern the other person raises. One cannot afford to overlook it, or worse still, trivialize it. 'Ah, don't even worry about such silly things' or 'Oh, such things never happen' are not what the customer wants to hear. If a doubt or a question or a concern has come up in their minds, they need to be assuaged with explanations and proof. If a concern persists, it is sure to come up again at some point in the remaining process or even after. This is why it's best to nip it in the bud.

Persuasion works best when we hold up a larger purpose in front of the customer.

Remember that people are more likely to respond with positive action when we hold up a mountain, not a molehill, for them to climb.

■

FISHY BUSINESS

When a customer voices concerns, it sometimes helps not to match logic for logic, but to answer with passion and counter with pride in your product.

ALTHOUGH I GREW UP in Odisha, my ancestors came from Bengal. To my knowledge, there are primarily three images that people associate with the state. The first is that of Goddess Kali – loving and annihilating at the same time, she is the quintessential woman herself. Second, and in that order, is the Bengali *bhadralok,* the man of the family, at once functioning with his head and his heart, both of which are located in his stomach. Third, which may be a bit difficult for a non-Bengali to fully appreciate, is the fish.

No Bengali household begins its day without the lady of the house sending the *bhadralok* to the *bajar* – which is a marketplace, close to but not the same as a bazaar – with two cloth bags, both well past their expiry dates, one for fresh produce and the other for fish. There, the *bhadralok* must buy his fish, every day, in small quantities according to the lady's strict requirements. This is because, in sensible households, refrigerated food is still looked down upon. We may be living in modern times, but refrigerated fish, at the very least, doesn't make the cut. The everyday trip to the *bajar* is also of some use to the *bhadralok* because it is his only form of exercise.

At the *bajar*, sellers of fresh vegetables and fish await the *bhadralok*'s arrival. There are dozens of fishmongers sitting with their wares, proudly extolling the superiority of what they are selling. Among the fishmongers, there is an active hierarchy. Those who sell the supreme fish, the hilsa or *ilish*, do not sell small carp, the *poonti*. Those who sell *galda chingdi*, oversized prawns that end where lobsters begin, don't sell *kucho chingdi*, the really tiny shrimp that are savoured for their flavour, not for their flesh.

Even though the buyers and sellers see each other every day, they go through the important ritual of haggling just as regularly, as if their lives depend on it. It is an act of devotion and not displeasure; it makes the somewhat pedestrian chore of buying and selling fish pleasurable and full of anticipation.

The first job of the *bhadralok* is to *not* buy any of the produce. He must leisurely, and with little regard for time, go around the entire *bajar*, pausing and reflecting at each fishmonger's stall, careful not to show active interest in any purchase. After the grand tour, he arrives at his chosen store, and even as the fishmonger welcomes him with a '*Babu, ashun*' ('Babu, come here'), the *bhadralok* must customarily ignore the greeting and get down immediately to business.

The haggling always begins with two objections: One, the quality of the fish and, two, the price. The first is handled with ferocity; the second debated with gentleness.

When the quality of the fish is questioned, the fishmonger challenges the *bhadralok* to poke the stomach of the fish. If soft, its tenderness suggests the onset of rot. At this point, if the buyer is still unimpressed, the fishmonger will pick up a fish, and even without a firm purchase order slit the animal's throat to show how red the blood from its gills is. That is the supreme evidence of gill quality and, therefore, of freshness.

After this, it is all about pricing.

There are three steps to the negotiation that follows:

The fishmonger will suggest X, but the buyer will counter with Y.

There is then a verbal dance around the two figures, albeit a short one. Both parties have other things to do. In reality, they know they are seeking point Z.

Nonetheless, the fishmonger knows better than to

jump the gun. By the end of it he or she will ask: '*Koto-te neben?*' ('How much would you like to pay?') That seminal question determines the price band within which point Z will rest and, soon after, the fish and money change hands.

There are days when fish are aplenty, the demand is low, and the *bhadralok* can afford to be stubborn. When the fishmonger knows this, he softens his stance. He lowers his margin. But the fishmonger will then also suggest that the *bhadralok* consider buying *galda chingdi*, the large succulent prawns with juicy heads, with the *ilish*, the delicate, tasty hilsa, even though the lady waiting at home may not have authorized the purchase. On these days, the cross-sale helps improve the lower margin because of the oversupply.

Every fishmonger of standing will have a sidekick, a partner who looks emaciated but is energetic, and who, for a fee, cuts the fish. After the active negotiation of the price from X to Y to Z, the fish is handed over to the cutter who then cleans and cuts the fish and must now get paid a fee.

This isn't a part of the deal. The *bhadralok*, now late for work and wary of the wrath he will have to face for overspending, pays the cutting charges and carries on.

∎

The fish-shopping expedition is not just about handling quality and price objections. Sometimes, buying fish is about things more cerebral.

When I heard my friend Sudip Banerjee was going to his hometown, Kolkata, I asked him to bring back some *eelish* with him. For a Bengali, an *ilish* handpicked in Kolkata is like a bottle of wine from the private cellar of a winegrower in Bourdeaux.

On his last day in Kolkata, Sudip was about to head to the fish market to pick up the good stuff when his father, who had heard about my request, decided to get into the act himself, saying that he couldn't trust Sudip's expertise. He insisted on going personally to get the fish 'that Subroto has so craved'.

So off went father and son to the market. As customary, the two men first made a reconnaissance of the entire market. At the very entrance was a middle-aged lady fishmonger, her red-bordered saree raised to her knees, cutting the head of a reasonably-sized *ilish* with the cutter's blade held between her toes. The old man asked her the going rate on the day in a matter-of-fact, non-committal manner. She replied that it was ₹500 for a kilo, and father and son moved on.

The fishmongers a little further inside the market sat higher in the pecking order than the lady. It was therefore to be assumed that they had better stuff, and would charge a premium for the quality of their product. As the two men trudged still deeper into the market, they came upon the still-bigger players; more shopkeepers than fishmongers, sellers who had both more fish, in variety and quantity, and more clout, with more impressive and permanent establishments. Then came the guys sitting on high platforms; these were the ones who were the biggest players, complete with assistants and all. As the two men went around, Sudip's father asked about the price for particular fish, which rose progressively but, strangely, the fish, both in quality and size, were comparable to what the lady at the gate was selling.

There had to be a catch somewhere, they thought to themselves. Sometime later, unable to solve the puzzle, they returned to her. How could she be selling her wares at a much lower price than those inside the *bajar*, Sudip's father demanded of her. The fish she stocked looked like they were of similar quality – were they not?

Busy removing scales off a large *ilish* on the cutter's blade for a waiting customer, she looked up and replied in a firm, almost reprimanding tone,'*Babu, kakhono kakhono goriber badi teyo sundari meye hoy.* (Sir, sometimes a pretty girl may be born even in a poor man's home.)

Her sharp repartee, witty and respectful at the same time, disarmed the old man completely; now he was beholden. They ordered the *ilish* and waited to be served.

The lady fishmonger had got it right. When a customer voices concern, it sometimes helps not to match logic for logic, but to answer with passion, counter with pride in your product, and sell it to them with all your heart.

THE LAST STRETCH TO 'YES'

In the end, how you handle the last lap decides the deal. Be authentic. Be transparent. Be confident. The job is not done till the paperwork is over.

EVERYONE WHO KNEW SATRAJIT Majumdar called him by his nickname, Benu-da. In his time, Benu-da was a legend, sought out by every cub in the office for real-time wisdom on anything to do with selling. Benu-da was a mechanical engineer who had sold pesticides when he began his working life and moved to the IT industry, where he was considered a pioneer. A long time ago, Benu-da and I, along with an ex-IBM executive named Sujit Bose, had started a company together: Project.21. When Project.21 folded up, we each went our separate ways but caught up occasionally whenever I came to Delhi, where Benu-da lived.

Sometime in the winter of 2015, Benu-da and I were meeting for a drink one evening at the India International

Centre (IIC) in Delhi. It was roughly around the time that this book was taking shape in my head. It was early by the standards of the members of the IIC, and we pretty much had the entire place to ourselves. It made for a quiet, personal space for the two of us. We took a table by the window and ordered some beer. It arrived quickly and I got right down to business.

I asked Benu-da his thoughts on the most defining moment in a sales cycle and what people find the most difficult to deal with.

He made no reply, lost in the tiny bubbles rising up in his glass of beer as if contemplating the creation of the universe. I repeated my question. He glanced at me in a way that indicated he had heard me the first time.

'Closing,' he said, after a pause. 'Asking for the order. That is the thing they find most difficult. Salespeople prospect. They qualify. They open a call. They handle all the objections. Then the moment of truth arrives. They need to close the deal, ask for the order, ask the prospect to become a customer by signing on the dotted line, and they fumble.'

'Why do you think that is?' I asked.

'Because they can't find an elegant way to say, "Now is the time, let's do it",' replied Benu-da simply. 'One of the difficulties of the act of closing is that it is intrusive by nature. Left to us, we don't like it when someone asks for closure, or worse still, demands it. Then there is the ultimate fear: the fear of rejection. The customer saying no.'

As Benu-da spoke, he turned around to catch the eye of an attentive server. The young man came to our table, his eagerness evident in his gait. 'Something to snack on, sir?' he asked.

Benu-da nodded, we ordered tandoori chicken tikka and the server bustled off.

'So how would you advise someone to go about it?' I asked. 'Closing, I mean?'

'Well, the basic thing to remember is not to rush in,' he replied meditatively a moment later. 'Salespeople need to make sure there are no unresolved issues pending before they close the deal. Address the issues first. Good salespeople go over a checklist with the customer and ensure that all the boxes are ticked – the customer's specific needs, any additional customization requested by them, actual costs, timelines, acceptance criteria, maintenance charges after the warranty period and the payment terms. They can then ask for the order.'

In a while, the smart young server came back to our table and asked if we were ready to decide what we would eat. As we looked at the menu, he suggested a few dishes he thought we might like to try. Benu-da asked for a serving of roast chicken and I settled for vegetable au gratin.

'In getting to the closing of the deal, one must watch the customer's body language,' Benu-da continued as the server moved away. 'If the customer is looking tense, quizzical or fidgety, it is a clear indication of discomfort. That discomfort needs to be addressed. If the client is appearing relaxed and happy, and greets you with a big smile, shakes your hand more firmly than before, clears up all his papers on his desk and takes out your proposal, it indicates a willingness to sign on the dotted line.'

'How can one tell how the customer is feeling about a deal?' I asked. 'Are there any signs apart from their body language that one should look out for?'

'Timing is important, too. You should not ask for the order too soon and certainly not after the moment has passed. One has to look for the signs; sometimes, the signs appear as questions.'

'Questions like?' I probed.

'For example, a customer might ask, "Are you convinced that the approach suggested by you in your updated proposal will work for us?" That indicates that they're on the fence, but willing to come over to your side if you can convince them. Or, it could be other issues. For example, they might say, "Your solution is certainly something that meets our needs but you are overpriced." Sometimes the client is concerned about how you intend to handle the stages after the agreement is signed. In that case, the questions might be something like: "Would you be open to a few changes if we wanted them?" or "How would you mobilize resources?" This tells you that the client is looking to move forward, but they're feeling uncertain about the next step. Reassurance is key, especially if you've already developed a good rapport with the client. They may even ask, "Will you be there personally to smoothen the inevitable initial hiccups?" or "Do you think we are ready for this?" These are both signs that the client is almost ready to sign.'

Benu-da, now less preoccupied and in full flow, continued: 'The customer may even indicate readiness. Questions such as "Who would head the programme implementation from your side? Can we meet the person?" or "Things look okay in your proposal to us but the boss has some reservations. Would you come along with me to clear things up?" are very good signs, in that sense.'

I nodded vigorously in agreement. Many among us don't realize one thing: that the customer may be saying the same things to another shortlisted party. However hard you may have worked to come this far, so – probably – has someone else. This, now, is the last lap. How you handle each question decides the fate of the deal. The customer wants to see you rise to the occasion. This is the moment for your show of confidence; not a time to be coy. You don't want to look like someone unprepared for success.

Benu-da was speaking again.

'In reality,' he said, 'there is no cookie-cutter approach to closing a deal because each time it is about human interaction. Each deal is unique, just as each customer and his needs are. But there are some things that never change. If I were to list them,' said Benu-da, counting on his fingertips, 'I would put them in this order. One, it is important to be authentic in what you say, and in how you present yourself. Authenticity is in short supply, hence high in demand. Two, every sales guy has the right to some embellishment, but this is not the time to exercise it. Closing a deal is a delicate, if not fragile, moment. You cannot display an anxiety to get it all done; your client's sole purpose in life isn't exactly to help you meet your sales quota. The important thing is to reassure the client that both of you have gone over all the points and are on the same page, remind them that they have made a good choice and then gently make the point that now is the time to shake hands. If they still seem uncertain, look them in the eye, smile, and ask if there is anything else you can do for them before the signing commences. And, finally, there is the signed paperwork. That is the most important thing of all. What they say is true: The job isn't done until the paperwork is over.'

Weeks after my conversation with Benu-da, I met a customer and the conversation led to Benu-da's statement about paperwork in a deal. At first, the customer laughed heartily, but the next moment he became serious and told me, 'But you know where some salespeople mess up? They do not show up after the paperwork is done. They leave the customer to chance after a customary "thank you" mail. Only the good ones come back after a month and then again after another month and then another, building a memorable association and ensuring recall.'

∎

THE
GRACIOUS
LOSER

The scope to improve, innovate and break new ground requires us to fail. If and when we do, the point is to handle it with tact, poise and brilliance.

MET NATALIE SMITH a good ten years ago in London when, one evening, somewhat at a loose end after a hectic week, I decided to go to the South Bank where an Indian dance troupe was to perform. She sat next to me during the show and, after the performance, I asked her what she did for a living. As it turned out, she was the business director of a European software company. I told her about Mindtree – she had already heard of the firm – and we exchanged business cards, and stayed in touch on and off.

After a few years of getting to know Natalie, I happened to be in London and gave her a call. She suggested dinner and fixed the venue – the Bibendum, a restaurant known for its modern French fare.

As we settled down, she laughingly showed me that the menu had the picture of the famous tire man, the unmistakable mascot of Michelin tires. When I confessed to being puzzled at finding the logo of a tyre company in a French restaurant, she laughed in agreement, and told me the story behind it.

Apparently, in the early 1900s, Michelin had dipped a toe into the restaurant guide book business, but with a specific reason in mind. At the time, there were perhaps only 3,000 cars in all of France. The two brothers who owned the tire company then had wanted people to drive more (if not buy more cars so that Michelin would sell more tyres), and for that noble purpose they had printed the first ever Michelin guide, which listed maps, tire repair and replacement instructions, car mechanics, hotels, and gas stations, and initially gave away some 35,000 copies for free. Eventually, though, they began to charge for the guides after they heard that a mechanic was using the guides to prop up a workbench, because 'man only respects what he pays for'. Today, of course, the firm has changed hands and the restaurant rating business is no longer owned by the tire company. But the Bibendum is located in a building that was once owned by them and served as the headquarters of the company in the United Kingdom. Hence the logo.

While telling her fascinating story, Natalie had chosen a lovely Chianti wine for me. After a sip of the full-bodied wine, the conversation veered towards how our careers had taken shape, about the ups and downs we'd been through and, somehow, we came to discuss the subject of failure, of losing a deal.

As it happened, Natalie had been working on a very large deal with an airline in Europe. The potential client had been looking at 'green field applications' that would keep it differentiated and competitive for the next five years. Deals like these take six to seven months, sometimes even as long as a year, to close. As one progresses through the various hoops of 'down-selection' – a process in which an initial list of 'possible vendors' is slowly culled down to a single 'chosen vendor' – the deal starts demanding more and more of your time.

At any rate, a time came when Natalie's company was neck-and-neck with the only other remaining vendor on the list. She had succeeded in putting together a very capable, high-powered team from the internal organization, and they had worked at the deal with sharp focus.

One day, the client called and told her that they had decided to give the two companies remaining in the fray the chance to do a proof-of-concept project, one that would last for six weeks. The proof-of-concept experience, the client had said, would help them make the final choice. With that, a new phase began and a delivery team was put together for the sole purpose of seeing the project through. With the business development people now out of the picture, there were no interlocutors.

After six weeks, Natalie learnt that the deal wasn't on their plate any more. The team that had been put on the proof-of-concept assignment had not quite measured up. The biggest reason given by the client was that the team, though proficient, didn't ask the client enough critical questions. They had simply delivered what was asked of them. The client felt that if a delivery team just went by specifications given to them and didn't question the assumptions behind the specifications, they wouldn't add any value to the final project.

Natalie sighed as she reached this part of the story. 'If only,' she said, 'I had taken the personal responsibility of ensuring that the team was picked right. If only I had flown down to spend time with them to get them contextually prepped.' She, and the rest of the leaders at her firm, had been so focused on winning the deal and on wooing the client that they had not paid attention to the internal realities.

By the time Natalie finished her story, the food arrived.

I told her that she was taking too much blame on herself. After all, wasn't the larger organization responsible for getting the deal executed?

'Yes,' she replied, 'but perhaps only when the deal is done.

You can't take your eyes off the ball because the deal isn't done yet. Actually, if I were to do it all over again, I would keep my eyes on the delivery execution for some time before declaring victory.'

I got the point she was making. Changing the topic, I asked her what she did when the client finally told her the deal was off.

She looked up from her food and told me she had written them an email – a 'nice email' is how she described it. 'I didn't want to say, as a sales team usually does, how disappointed we were, or seed fear, uncertainty and doubt in their minds about the guys who won and end by saying we were there should something not work out.'

This was new. What she had done was not standard practice among sales organizations. I quickly jumped at the opportunity. 'I want to read this letter you wrote,' I said. 'Not many people know how to lose well.'

She smiled at my reaction and agreed to send it to me. 'You know what,' she said, 'a couple of weeks after I sent the mail, I got a reply from the CIO of the client organization, the boss overseeing the selection process. He wrote saying he had made a strong recommendation to a subordinate in his previous company who was looking for a new supplier. And we did win that one!'

When Natalie's mail reached me, I knew immediately what had won her organization the recommendation from a client who had decided not to work with them.

Dear _____,

I'm writing to thank you for considering us in your partner selection process for the next-generation IT project. We have been very impressed by the RFP selection process that your team ran. All of us enjoyed every part of the engagement. In this mail, I want to share our thoughts on both the process as well as what we learned along the way about your company and your team.

- Your team was empowered; they shifted through the gears very efficiently at different stages, without your being directly involved.

- We felt it was a comprehensive, well-thought-out process, with enough quality time available for us to engage meaningfully with your team and articulate our proposition well. There seemed to be a clear focus on listening deeply and probing the depth of capability and seriousness of intent of potential partners without, at any time, talking down or being remotely adversarial in any way.

- From our vantage point, it seemed the emphasis was on a careful understanding of capability, rather than on transference of risk to a vendor. This gave us the reassurance needed to engage deeply with your team.

- The involvement of various team members at different stages of the process showed a focus on collaboration within the organization as well as on change management and getting the buy-in of various stakeholders who would work with any partner eventually chosen.

- Across the board, we saw clear signals of an open, collaborative and well-grounded culture. From the meetings in the conference room to sharing your thoughts with us, from the way the team set the tone of the engagement to the way _____ and _____ interacted with our various teams during their visit to us, just to cite a few examples, we saw consistent and clear evidence of this culture.

- We felt the pilot engagement was a well-thought-out exercise that examined our capabilities in a real-world setting, as it were, with a well-scoped problem statement that lent itself to being delivered over the two Sprints.

- There was a clear focus on engineering excellence, as well as technical collaboration – both seemed as important as the end-product of the Sprints.

- There was a very strong emphasis on Agile principles right through the exercise – the continuous feedback and constant engagement; the diligence around 'Inspect and Adapt'; the story-sizing principles; daily stands; testing approach; the use of use case, etcetera.

- The discussions on Architecture were also illuminating, with focus on the end solution and on thinking of extensibility, NFRs and potential changes well in advance.

- Collaboration was, of course, a clear theme right through the exercise.

_____, I would be dishonest to say we are not disappointed that we didn't make the cut. But, given the process and content your team followed, we have no doubts that, all things considered, you have made a good choice. Given your culture of open collaboration and clarity of thought, it will be a privilege for anyone to be your partner and I am sure, together, your organization will succeed in a big way. On our part, we will look forward to any potential opportunity that could come up outside of your current frame of engagement.

In closing, please thank everyone in your team for the excellent cooperation, openness and fair dealing extended to us at every step.

Warm regards,

Natalie Smith

In sales, we obsess about winning. In truth, the scope to improve, to innovate and break new ground requires us to fail. But even as we deal with the occasional, inevitable failure, we gloss over them. In typical sales meets and conferences, the wins are given exaggerated attention and the losses are quickly buried under justifications and, sometimes, in a pointless blame game. To steer clear of this route and keep the big picture at the centre of one's vision, one has to develop a reflective space, have the ability to step back and be authentic. Finally, there may always be failure that needs to be handled; the point is to handle it with tact, poise and brilliance.

■

BE THERE
OR
BE SQUARE

Good news can arrive by mail; bad news must be delivered in person.

THE ENCOUNTER I HAD with the barman at the Marriott Hotel in Washington DC, recounted in the chapter titled 'Raising the Bar', was around the time we were pitching to Bruce Hoffmeister, the Chief Information Office (CIO) of Marriott Hotels.

Bruce is one of my all-time favourite customers because of many reasons; one among them is his fairness. Ever since we have known each other in the course of doing business, we have suffered a major setback just once. At the time, it fell to me to break the news of damages, delays and consequences to him. It wasn't a pleasant duty.

Over the next few days, teams on both sides worked hard and brought the situation under control. As it unfolded, we tracked the process of problem resolution in the same way that Cape Kennedy would tackle a problem reported on a spaceship. Fortunately, we put out the fire but, later, when everyone had a breather, the teams assembled and we did what we call a system relive, complete with a root-cause analysis and a workshop on the lessons that had been learnt from the experience. The following day, I got on the phone with Bruce to thank him for everything. That is when he said something to me that I will always remember. He said, 'Sometimes things will go wrong. Horribly wrong. We all make mistakes.' Then he said sagely, 'No one expects you to be perfect. But you will be judged for your response to the situation.'

His words made me think. We are neurologically wired to seek happiness. We don't like adversity, however much the gurus and the scriptures eulogize their latent and obvious benefits. Yet, life is what it is. No one's life is complete without, at one time or another, having to deal with a situation that has gone wrong and then having to convey the unpleasant news to the client. The range of bad news can be anything from a delayed delivery to a defective product, a key employee leaving or a system crash with a sizable business impact.

In times like these, the few things that matter the most are authenticity, timeliness, assurance and follow-through.

Adversity is often the test that singles out the trusted advisors from the salespeople.

The crux of authenticity is straightforwardness. For this, one needs to put oneself in the customer's shoes. If the laundry service you use has burnt a hole in your Pashmina shawl, you don't want some evasive nonsense or excuses being spouted. You need the news to be broken to you as is. If the courier has lost your parcel, you want to know the situation clearly, without any embellishments. If the medicine a doctor has prescribed for your child is showing a negative reaction, the medical team needs to tell you straight, without using jargon, what the matter is and the treatment plan ahead.

Customers put their reputation at risk when their vendors fail to deliver on a promise. It is a delicate moment for them. That is when we have to ask: 'What if this happened to me? What if the bad news had consequences for me?'

If it is indeed bad news for the other person, tell it as it is. Don't try to sugarcoat it, don't dance around the issue, and don't fake it, even slightly. And don't hide behind an email or an SMS. Be there in person. If that is not possible, pick up the phone and speak. As I like to say it, good news can arrive by mail; bad news must be delivered in person.

■

If I were to list the 12 things to do after conveying bad news to a client, they would be:

ALLOW TIME for the news to sink in.

IF THERE IS AN OUTBURST, take it. It is not against you. Those angry feelings have to be let out before reason can return and you can be of further help. Outbursts are a good thing, and it's best not to interrupt when the client is venting.

AFTER THE INITIAL REACTION, say that you are sorry, that you know and realize how the other person feels. In that moment, own the mess, even if it isn't your doing. Be straightforward about the implications, the downsides of whatever has gone wrong. Be clear about the particulars you give: How long will it be before things return to normal? What will shut down? Who and what services may be impacted and by what degree of inconvenience?

YOUR BODY LANGUAGE AND VOICE, in person, over a video call or on the phone, must convey three things: Concern, Competence and Confidence.

CONVEY A MITIGATION PLAN, however incomplete or simplistic it may be. It is the first response and speed matters. Inform the client what you are doing about the problem, what internal and external expertise is being summoned to salvage the situation. Put names and faces on the expertise. If it is an oil well fire, for instance, it better be the likes of the late fire-fighting icon Paul Neal 'Red' Adair. Basically, nothing but the best will do.

MANY A TIME, what you may be delivering is breaking news – that is, it is incomplete since the situation is still unfolding; you do not know the full story yet. Even so, tell the client however much you do know. Reassure them that you will come back as soon as you have learnt something new, and come back you must, even if nothing new has come up. Don't get lost in the ether after the first communication just because there isn't anything new to report.

ASK THE CUSTOMER FOR ADVICE and help. Often, salespeople underestimate their ability and willingness to join forces against the adversity.

AT EACH INTERVENTIONAL MOMENT, publish the risks you see for the path chosen and how you plan to deal with them, along with the trade-offs, and get the client's approval on all of this. In bad times, surprises aren't that welcome.

COMMUNICATE. Communicate. Communicate. Communicate – right through the life of the disaster. Do so in person or on the phone rather than by text or email.

WHEN DAMAGES ARE KNOWN and business loss has occurred, offer to bear the pain. Depending on the nature of your product, you could replace equipment, rebuild broken systems at no extra charge, provide credit against future purchases, work in a total refund – whatever it takes to show that you are an equal partner.

DON'T JUST MOVE ON after the 'oil spill' is cleaned up. Send a formal, final report to the client on the root causes, lessons learnt and the future course of action.

AND – ALWAYS – GO BACK ONE MORE TIME to say how sorry you are for whatever has happened. One day, it will stand you in good stead.

■

THINKING
OF
YOU

The successful culmination of any job is the outcome of collaborative work on many fronts. Being grateful to each of those fronts for having worked to their potential (or beyond) can lead to further success and fruitful alliances.

Lu ELLEN IS AN award-winning cross-cultural consultant and has been training global teams of high-tech and pharmaceutical corporations in Asia, Europe, the Middle East and the Americas for many years now. Lu Ellen's personal and professional passion is to lead best-practice sessions on how to work effectively, and efficiently with geographically and culturally diverse teams.

I first met Lu Ellen in 1991 in the Bay Area in California, where I had been deputed to set up Wipro's R&D business in the Silicon Valley. While the company's R&D engineers were great, they did not have training in cross-cultural issues and that, we knew, could come in the way of professional effectiveness. I approached the University of California for help. At the time, cross-cultural training programmes existed for Japanese executives doing business in the United States and vice versa, but there was nothing on the Indo-American front, and the university commissioned Lu Ellen to design and deliver a programme for Wipro engineers who were new to the United States. In the decades to follow, business exploded between India and the United States, as did the demand for Lu Ellen's training.

Over the years, Lu Ellen became like a member of my family. Whenever we met we had long, engaging conversations about global business that inevitably boiled down to people, to human beings across the planet, and how they engaged with each other on the business fora. The one thing that I have observed Lu Ellen being very particular about in her training is the need to express gratitude and say 'thank you'. She does it every day, even as she is globetrotting, and each time in a very individualized, personal and thoughtful manner. She believes that gratitude is a very powerful emotion, and in my life, too, I have never been in doubt about that.

During the last conversation we had, I told Lu Ellen about Dr Edward Hoffman, a well-known psychology professor at Yeshiva University in New York City, and his views on the powerful nature of gratitude. Dr Hoffman is widely respected for his thoughts on mental health and well-being in a larger context and his writing appears on the portal of White Swan Foundation, a not-for-profit organization for mental health that I have co-founded. According to him, expressing gratitude goes well beyond a mere 'thank you' conveyed to someone who has done us a good turn, given us a referral, issued a repeat purchase order, and the like. It helps, he says, to make a 'gratitude list', or to keep a 'gratitude journal', and that it is important to write letters to those to whom you wish to express gratitude. In general, he recommends that people be committed to practising gratitude.

On hearing that, Lu Ellen smiled and told me a simple thing: 'We often forget how many acts, intended to convey thoughtfulness, can actually end up being ordinary, sometimes crass. A text message sent on someone's birthday, with wishes for a great year ahead, could come across as superficial. Sometimes people do not customize their messages. It is a mass blast and a tacky best wishes message accompanied by a downloaded emoji. People can figure out when they're being mass-mailed. Even if you do customize your message, there is this pedestrian way some people do it. A mail beginning with "Dear Subroto and family" tells you from a mile away that it is machine-speak; it is a cut-and-paste job or just a mail-merge, right?'

I nodded in agreement. For someone who receives as many emails and messages as salespeople do on an average day, mass-mailed messages are more of an irritation to be got rid of than an expression of genuine thoughtfulness.

'Salespeople,' she added, 'need to be thoughtful.'

'What would you say separates a thoughtful message from one that is superficial?' I asked.

'There are many ways of expressing gratitude,' she replied. 'These could range from a thank-you card, a gift hamper during the holiday season, or a book gifted to a client on a subject that interests them. But what touches people is not an impersonal card saying 'thank you'. What works much better is something personal; for example, imagine you wanted to express gratitude to a large client who has just cleared a big project for you. Think of sending a handwritten letter, written on handmade paper, asking the client to suggest a charity of choice to which your organization would make a humble contribution this coming holiday season. Now, a thing like that is thoughtful. The key is to always be genuinely thinking about hundreds of such ways in which you can express yourself and, in the process, tell the client you were really thinking of him.

'Think of it this way: Instead of simply asking the customer out for dinner, offer to host an offsite for a joint team from both sides and request the customer to speak to them. This goes beyond superficial gratitude and expresses an honest emotion. It conveys thoughtfulness, respect and the desire to work together; it expands the glory as you create a platform for the client to be heard.'

'Of course,' I said, thinking of the ways I had dealt with similar situations, but Lu Ellen had more to share.

'I often get video links from people I know,' she continued. 'Or suggestions on good books and articles to read. Nonetheless, very few people personalize their messages. For example, very rarely do people say something like, "Lu Ellen, do you remember that we had a conversation in your office a few weeks ago? I have been thinking about it and, in that context, I found this excellent video that I think is worth your time. The video is a little long but engaging right through. You can keep it in the 'to-view' list for the weekend and do let me know thoughts on it." A personalized message makes all the difference.

'If you're sending someone a gift, don't just pick something up thoughtlessly. Send something handmade you picked out as the artisan was making it and, in the process, you convey, "I was thinking of you." People know when you think particularly of them.'

Reflecting for a moment, Lu Ellen turned to me. 'Now let me ask you something. What about thanking people in your own organizations without whose help you can't win a deal? How do you go about that?' she asked.

I paused, and admitted, 'Well, I think we take them for

granted. As soon as the deal has landed, we quickly move on. It's easy to say everyone's got busy, no one has the time.'

'Yes, I do find that in most organizations,' said Lu Ellen. 'It doesn't take much time, you know, just a little focused attention. Think of the person in the legal department who pushed your contract through quicker than usual because he knew it was important to you. He stayed back late in office three nights in a row to do it. Sure, you could say that it is his job. However, he didn't have to go the extra mile, but he did. So what would be important to him? How about movie passes for his family? He can make it a special family night by taking his three kids out for a movie and some popcorn. What about the pre-sales engineer who rescued you in a meeting? She saved the day by showing the client how your idea was a good one when you realized in a panic that your presentation was not hitting the mark. A thoughtful email to her manager detailing how crucial her input was may make a good deal of difference to her performance review.'

She paused, then said, 'Tell them exactly what it was they did that you appreciate. Tell them what their work means to you.'

These were sobering thoughts. It came to my mind that saying 'thank you' is often a mechanical act, a formality, but gratitude is a feeling. Whenever we feel grateful to someone or for something, it is preceded by a moment of mental calm.

This is, in itself, therapeutic. The successful culmination of any job, sales-related or otherwise, is the outcome of collaborative work on many fronts, and being grateful to each of those fronts for having worked to their potential (or beyond) can lead to further success and fruitful alliances. Personally, for me, the idea of gratitude has greatly impacted my life and work. Not a day goes by without me realizing how many people have collaborated throughout my life to bring me to where I am today. And that includes Lu Ellen.

■

DO IT LIKE THE SWEDES

Increasingly, customers observe the culture of the seller company not through the sales pitches it makes, nor the corporate slide deck, but by opening the lid and looking into its everyday life.

O N ONE OF MY trips back from the United States, I stopped over at Gothenburg in Sweden for a day. The place has always fascinated me. From the time Mindtree won Volvo as an account in the days of the company's infancy, I have had the chance to visit the historic city – now the country's second-most populous city – quite a few times. It used to be a ship-building centre and has a character of its own with its history of Dutch merchants and Scotsmen, and its great maritime past. Today, it has no more to do with ships than the last big ship manufactured in the city being anchored permanently on the river, serving as a car park.

As much as I have loved Gothenburg for its quaintness, I have always respected the Swedish people for their egalitarian values, their respect for individuals and their attitude to many aspects of doing business. Early in our relationship with Volvo, we began to pay attention to the Swedish way of looking at the world, and that careful attention has won us more business elsewhere, especially in the other Nordic countries.

It is only after we started working with the Swedes that we started to internalize the fact that large and enlightened customers everywhere are beginning to look at big-ticket purchase decisions very differently. Given the fact that the buyer has a global brand and the ticket size of a deal may be large, the buyer knows it can pretty much pick any partner that would deliver high-quality goods and services at competitive prices. Hence, while making a choice, the focus has become the innate character of the would-be service or goods provider, the value the provider can add beyond the deal on the table and how its reputation can be an asset to the buyer. Hence, what you sell becomes different from simply eulogizing the product or service you may have on the tray. The conversation is based largely on the very amorphous thing called culture. So, how do you put that on display?

People observe the culture of a company not in the sales pitches made, nor the corporate slide deck, but by opening the lid of the company and looking into its everyday life. The more you facilitate that process, the greater becomes the comfort level between you and the customer. Customers look at the dynamics at work. Early in the conversation, they look at how hierarchical a company is – the more pronounced the hierarchy, the higher will be the communication overheads at the time that the actual relationship begins.

Andre Nicholas, our coach in the early days of our selling to the Swedes, had told me that most companies would simply field the top guys in pitching a deal. That is a folly. When you put junior employees forward to place the deal, make them the front end of your presentations, it gives the buyer the chance to get to know what is really on offer. After all, it is these people who will run the show after the deal is won. Quite often, junior executives are not sent forward because there is a lingering worry about them making a mistake. If someone from the customer's side asks a question, the senior-most person from the provider's side jumps in, instead of letting the person with the expertise, however junior he may be, answer. That smacks of hierarchy and it leaps out at the buyer.

Speaking of hierarchy, the customers notice even the subtlest of signals that point to a healthy work culture. The way they perceive it is: if a junior person from your side is contradicting a senior employee, it indicates empowerment.

The buyer gauges how much dissent and expression of individual opinion is practised in your company. They then use their observations to arrive at conclusions about the conflict management abilities and resolution processes at the provider's end because they know that conflicts are inevitable.

They are also constantly looking for signs of inclusion, equality and actions towards sustainability as signs of a progressive and mature organization. Even as you think they are viewing the sleek corporate video playing before them, their eyes are soaking in the tell-tale signs of diversity and awareness. Is your team mostly male? Are the women seated far away, playing second fiddle? Are your premises only symbolically handicap-enabled or have you gone beyond the ramp? Are you aware of your carbon footprint and consciously working towards lowering it over time? Or do you not really care?

It's important, Andre told us, to admit to your past mistakes, discuss how you recovered from them and what you learnt in the process. Equally crucial is the need to showcase your organization's governance standards, not just in the way a project is managed but in the way the organization is run on a day-to-day basis. That becomes a big clincher.

Alongside the serious issues, they are also looking for how much fun it will be to work with you. How much your people laugh is a critical aspect of how stress-free the relationship is going to be.

Today, it is not just the Swedes who function this way. From the United States to Japan, and in India itself, progressive organizations are embracing a different set of behaviours that are beginning to influence their internal culture. A company's culture is no longer a fringe issue. Customers want to buy products and services with a certain culture at its core. If that core appears incompatible with their own, they will look elsewhere. If the new world imperatives that your organization has embraced are not yet in your organization's messaging and are absent from your sales tool kit, it is perhaps time you called on someone like Andre.

■

THE CHAMPION

What does it take to be a champion seller?

A VERY LONG TIME ago, somewhere in ancient China, there was a village where archers of great capability met once a year to fiercely compete with each other. At the end of the day, one of them would be crowned the champion. It was considered the greatest honour of the day.

The participants came from faraway places, where they had practised for an entire lifetime to compete for the ultimate honour. A grand jury watched the competition with keen attention to choose the best of the best. But this contest wasn't just about defeating one's rivals and emerging as the most skilled of them all. One had to be perfect, not simply the best, in order to win the championship. Thus, there were years when no individual would qualify as the champion even though one among those who had come to compete was clearly the best.

The mysterious thing about it was that the jury never explained what exactly it took to be declared a champion.

One year, a young and highly accomplished archer came to the competition. As the event progressed, he defeated all his rivals one after another, and came to stand in front of the jury. The jury huddled together to deliberate in a circle; he couldn't quite follow their discussions but waited patiently. Then came the moment of reckoning. The head juror announced that that year, no one was going to be declared the champion.

This infuriated the young man, and he demanded to know what he lacked. Why, after excelling in every task assigned to him, was he not being awarded the title of champion? If they didn't want to tell him, he said, they should point him to a living champion, if there was any at all. He would meet this champion and judge for himself.

At that, they went into another huddle.

After what seemed like an eternity, the head juror returned. He said, 'Young man, the last person to be crowned champion resides on top of a mountain far away. You can go and meet him if you are ready for a long ordeal.'

The young archer took note of the champion's whereabouts and set off on his course.

After days and months of arduous trekking up many mountains, he finally arrived at his destination. But, to his dismay, he found no one there. Frustrated, he began to search the place, suspecting trickery. Then, just as his anger was about to boil over, he noticed a frail figure lying under a tree.

He approached the person somewhat in desperation. The man was barely conscious, but the young traveller nudged him until he opened his eyes. The old man squinted his eyes to focus on the youth, and asked in a whisper who he was and what he was seeking.

'I have come in search of the champion,' the young man replied. Then he narrated the story of the archery competition, and explained why he had travelled so far.

After listening to the entire story, the old man said in a feeble voice, 'I am the champion you seek.'

The young man was shocked. A man, who could not raise himself from the ground, who was almost dying of frailty – how could he be the champion?

The old man then pointed at the bow and arrows the young man was carrying, and asked what they were. The young man was shocked, but he explained their purpose. The old man showed him a flock of birds flying high up in the sky and asked him bring one down.

'Which one?' the young man asked.

'The third one from the lead bird on the right flank,' replied the old man feebly.

The young man took aim, pulled the string to bend the bow and released the arrow.

The bird fell.

'Now it's your turn,' the young man said, offering him his bow and arrows.

'Which one?' asked the old man.

'Bring the last bird down,' said the young man.

To this, the old man pointed his finger skyward and asked, 'You mean that one there?'

And by the time the young man had nodded his assent, the bird had fallen to the ground.

■

The man who told me the story is Rajeev Sawhney. He and I started on our sales careers at roughly the same time. We spent a lot of time exploring territories, selling together, being each other's prep boards before a big call. We also had a lot of fun together. It was a trusted relationship. In the ensuing years, our paths diverged but whenever we met we picked up from where we had left off.

Rajeev's career in sales started with selling garments in a funky shop in Delhi that catered to teenagers with an irreverent brand name like FU's in the early eighties. From there, he went on to selling computer hardware and then complex digital solutions globally and eventually reached the pinnacle of his sales organization.

I called Rajeev up after a long time and both of us laughed, remembering the story of the champion.

'Tiger,' I said, calling Rajeev by his popular nickname, 'this time I've come to you with a purpose. I want the champion to tell me what it takes to be a champion at selling.'

'Remember the birds in the story?' Rajeev asked. 'Let us take the birds down, one by one, to arrive at the answer. How about that?'

'I'm game,' I said.

Rajiv is a methodical, meticulous thinker, and a thunderous orator if he chooses to be one. Counting them off on his fingertips, these are the qualities of a champion seller that he identified:

BIRD 1   THE ONE THAT HAS A STRATEGY TO WIN

If you want to build a great career as a salesperson, you've got to read a lot. Read up on history, read up on science, read about cultures and music and the minds of geniuses. Salespeople need to be informed and interesting at all times, and reading is the best way to keep abreast and up to date. Most salespeople give up on reading by the time they hit mid-career and, after that, it is very difficult to build back the habit. When you don't read, you lose the ability to tell stories – and isn't the skill of telling a good story the key to successful selling? A lot of selling must be approached from a strategic point of view. That is why books on strategy are my favourites, and chief among them is *The Art of War* by Sun Tzu. From it I learnt that it is not enough to win; you should be able to do so without exerting yourself excessively. A skilful player is able to win without having to put up a lengthy operation in the field and put in too much effort. You don't want to be left tired after the victory, you know. Did you see how effortlessly the champ brought the bird down? He may have been frail, but his skill and efficiency had not deserted him.

When salespeople exhaust themselves by exerting a lot, they cannot play for very long. Once you learn to be effortless, you can be in the field for a longer period of time. You can give yourself more time to plan. You can create the white space to build strategy to outsmart your competition. Salespeople who exert too much also end up exerting their own support system in the organization. The best way to be effortless is to plan well, stay informed, choose your turf wisely and be prepared to play the long game.

BIRD 2   THE ONE THAT KNOWS WHERE TO PLAY AND HOW TO WIN

Don't be all over the place. I remember the time when Barrack Obama had been elected president of the United States. Everyone was talking about energy conservation, about smart grids. The company I worked for had as little idea about smart grids as anyone else. We sensed it was going to be big, but the key was to move in quickly. We did that and landed some really big deals. Remember the Bob Dylan song "Blowin' in the Wind"? It's like that; you've got to blow "in" the wind. If the winds are blowing in a particular direction, all you need to do is to adjust the sail in your boat so that you start moving in that direction. The point, though, is to be selective and wise. Every wind that blows may not take you in the direction of success; to recognize the ones that will, you will first have to have superb knowledge of the capabilities of your boat and how flexible it's sail really is.

BIRD 3   THE ONE WHOSE MOTTO IS 'PREPARE, PREPARE, PREPARE'

The better prepared you are, the more likely you are to succeed. Anticipation is the key. This requires a certain rigour and discipline. For every deal, anticipate the questions, anticipate the objections, anticipate the competitive scenario and anticipate the influence map. Consider what new requirements might come up, what obstacles may emerge. Anticipation is the starting point of all preparation. I demand that from my team and my colleagues, and I don't get into a meeting until a good amount of preparation has gone in and I'm fully satisfied with the preparation that has been done.

BIRD 4   THE ONE THAT AIMS FOR WIN, WIN, WIN

This may sound very straightforward, but a lot of salespeople have stumbled in the long run because all they wanted was to have a single win, one in which they alone have succeeded. In every win, there must actually be three wins. The real champions are those who know this. When you conclude the deal, your customer must win, your company must win and, most importantly, the individuals involved in the customer organization that steered the deal must win. If the three wins are not aligned, then you are bound to have a mishap sooner or later and the win will not be sustainable. When you make the individual who shepherded the deal a winner, that person remembers it; people move on and change jobs, and you are bound to get called again.

BIRD 5   THE ONE THAT DOESN'T LOSE SIGHT OF THE PURPOSE OF THE PURSUIT

I often find people getting carried away in making that one great presentation. They forget that the purpose is to make the sale and not the presentation. The presentation may well be a distraction. The purpose is the central theme around which you build your pursuit, your grand plan. You cannot let the other activities in the Brownian Movement become the things that distract you, engulf you and make you lose sight of the purpose you are really after.

BIRD 6   THE ONE THAT NEVER LOSES THE STORY

You will have the wins and the losses, but you have to be mindful to never lose the story. In every win and, more so, in every loss, there is a powerful lesson. That lesson holds the key for major future successes. But it waits to be sought. People quickly move on from one success or failure to the next opportunity. They don't pause to reflect. I think anybody doing that is committing a crime because introspection is valuable. It will prevent you from suffering further loses. It will enhance the win ratios.

BIRD 7   THE ONE WHO IS LIKE THE OLYMPIAN, SERGEY BUBKA

Sergey Nazarovych Bubka, the Ukrainian pole vaulter, beat his own world record several times, year after year – he did this precisely fourteen times. Bubka is *that* champion, the classic example that teaches us to learn to excel and better our own record in whatever we do. Many salespeople, after tasting success, glide into comfortable complacency and hence into mediocrity because they do not perceive a threat to their position as the best in the game. Remember, when there is no other competition, you've got to do a Bubka.

BIRD 8   THE ONE THAT TAKES THE BROAD VIEW

Don't harbour a myopic view of the customer. Many salespeople have a myopic view of a deal. Some say that a client has a requirement of five people to work as contractors on a project; someone else says that the client just wants to build a small application for which he needs people to test the platform. These are examples of myopic thinking. A champion will ask: *Why? Why is the customer asking for these specifics?* I have a golden rule: Ask "why" seven times and you will arrive at what is driving the customer's need. In the process, you may unravel a much bigger programme behind it and realize that it is not just a small project that the client needs your company's expertise on. There may be a much bigger opportunity for you here. That realization can suddenly change the landscape, altering the scale of the opportunity and what you need to seed. Often, I have uncovered large deals behind something as innocuous and innocent as a tiny staffing project. A champion believes in looking at the programme beyond the project.

BIRD 9   THE ONE THAT KILLS THE FEAR

As professionals, all of us have our fears. We may not show them; sometimes we may be in denial about them, and at other times we may not even be aware of them. But every such fear leads us to underperform. For example, a salesperson may be afraid of losing, hence they avoid negotiations. Perhaps they don't read enough, so they avoid making calls to customers who may be knowledgeable. Or they may be fearful of making presentations, so they insist that the technical people go along with them every time and in the process miss many opportunities because the technical team isn't always there to tag along.

So how do you kill your fear?

Read up. This sounds counter intuitive, but it is true that reading dispels fear. For instance, you meet a prospect for the first time and they use three words in a meeting you have never heard before. You have to meet them again next week and you feel awkward going for the meeting without your technical expert. You don't need to get fazed. Spend a few hours reading about what you do not know and you will see your fear vanish. There are so many good books on every possible subject, and if you are able to filter out the clutter then the Internet, too, is a storehouse of knowledge and information.

Practise like hell. When fear presents itself before you in the form of that large client meeting in which six of their experts will sit down to create a short list of three providers who will receive the RFP from the ten who have pitched for the business, what you need is practise. Practise the entire sequence over and over and over again. Practise alone and practise with the full team. Unravel your fear and go after it. Practise is the sunlight that burns right through the fog of fear.

BIRD 10   THE ONE THAT COMMUNICATES EFFECTIVELY

You may be the best at what you do, but if you cannot communicate your skill, you cannot sell it. The communication I am speaking of is not the spoken word. It refers to your personality, your presence on the Internet, your keen sense of observation and the quality of your silence when the customer is speaking. These are all vehicles of communication. Only the best communicators deliver the story effectively. As you will see, people do not care about much else. They care for the story.

■

ON A
CONCLUDING
NOTE

PEOPLE WHO SELL WELL are a joy. They sell without needing to sell. The way they go about 'selling' elevates the act to the point where they are serving a customer's needs. They make us happy, they make us grateful. We look forward to meeting them again, to buying from them again. Our relationships with them become ones that we cherish.

Take, for instance, my most favourite photo framer in the world. Her name is Veena. She has a small workshop tucked away off the Nandi Durg Road in Bengaluru. In most part, she restores period furniture and knick-knacks for art lovers. One part of her workshop, however, is devoted to photo framing. A few months ago, I had taken to her an old cloth embroidered by my mother that was in a state of disrepair.

I asked her to frame it for me. She took one look at it and asked me to take the cloth to INTACH.

'This is so precious,' she said. 'At INTACH, they should be able to restore it after which we will frame it. If I just frame it for you, it will last a couple of decades. If they restore it first, it will last a lot longer.'

I took her advice and approached INTACH. They took a few months to return it after a thorough restoration job. After that I brought it back to Veena and requested her to frame it for me. I have never had to tell Veena how to frame my pictures. She advises me on the many options I have and quite often warns me against something I may have chosen, something on which she could have probably made twice the amount of money.

As with Veena, I have another great relationship with the person who sells me seeds and saplings for my garden. His name is Susanta Das and he has a small store selling garden and farm supplies in Bhubaneswar. Whenever he calls me, I jump with joy. We talk about this and that – how the gladiola are doing and whether the neem cakes he had suggested worked to rid the lawn of white ants. But even as he speaks, I actually lose patience because I just want him to tell me about the new arrivals at his store and what I can add to my garden. Unhurriedly, he gets there. He has some late-blooming lilies, he says, and some gerbera that will bloom year-long. How many does he have and can he please keep aside a hundred of each for me, I ask. And so our exchanges continue. On matters of shrubs and trees and everything in between, Susanta has become a trusted advisor to me. At the crux of the relationship are his professional knowledge, his respect for his customers and his pleasant dealings. But, most crucially, he cares about what finally happens after his customer carries home a seedling or a bulb. The transaction of buying and selling between us is an incidental process that facilitates the blooming bud.

Then there is my favourite photo printer in Bengaluru. His name is Venkatesh. For as long as I have known him, he has been producing high-quality prints for studios, artists and designers, and amateurs like me who think a relationship with him upgrades them to being seen as 'pros'. He can look at an image and tell you what paper you should print it on. 'Use a museum print for this one,' he will say. Or 'This will work well on a canvas.' Periodically, I book an appointment with him, like booking an appointment with a doctor. I don't want anything distracting him when we are meeting. I take my photographs along, upload them on his system, and then we look at them together and settle for a size and type of paper on which to print them. The process often takes hours. In the end, I realize I had brought two dozen more images that we didn't have the time to look at. I leave them behind with him and ask him to take a look at them at his own pace, choose the ones he feels will look good enlarged and make decisions on the print sizes. Later, I call him, ask him the amount I owe him and send a cheque. He offers a service, like many others, but he does so with admirable dedication and professionalism.

I have never talked to Veena, Susanta and Venkatesh about price. I don't negotiate with them and I feel as though asking them for a discount would be an insult to the mutual trust we have. It is actually more than trust; it is friendship of a very special kind. I consider them my trusted advisors and hugely respect them for their knowledge. Each time I speak to them or meet them in person, I am eager to buy something from them. I feel restless until they let me do so. Each time we settle the dues, I go over their bills to make sure they haven't forgotten to add something I asked for at the last moment, had picked up but hadn't paid for. In reality, I want to make sure that they are not under-charging me. They are truthful, honest, authentic, pleasant and fun to be around. There is something that gives me a sense of supreme comfort when I am with them. I know they will never sell anything to me that they would not buy for themselves.

Everyone has such people in their lives. A dentist you take your child to. A guy who tunes your favourite, all-carbon, racing bicycle that you don't let anyone touch. A fruit seller or fishmonger, a hairdresser, an architect, a software engineer, a shoe-repairer, a bookseller or a neighbourhood chef – anyone whose ability to sell you something of value gives you great joy.

I have done many deals in my life as a businessman; I have, as you know by now, tremendous pride in my basic ability to sell. I consider it my defining, core skill. In that ability, I hope the many people I have done business with feel the same way about me as I feel about Veena, Susanta and Venkatesh.

■

THANK YOU

Grateful thanks are due to a lot of people, but chief among them is to my editor, Poulomi Chatterjee. Without her, this book would not have seen the light of day. Here is a confession: More than once, during the writing of the book, I had lost hope. I had moments of serious self-doubt as a writer. Poulomi not only got this book out of me but also gave my thoughts new life.

I also want to acknowledge with deep gratitude all the 'Druids' I have spoken about and quoted in this book, for having shared their formulae for success and fulfilment so joyfully. In presenting them up close, I wanted to remind my readers that their counterparts are present in every organization. The trick is to take note of them, approach them for guidance so that they may part with the secrets of their effectiveness.

While the lessons from all the Druids are real, the settings have sometimes been fictionalized. Remember that I had told you right at the beginning that the story is important? Now don't go looking for actual evidence.

And, finally, thank you, dear reader, for buying this book. I hope it will help you to refine your game at work and life in many ways.

■

THE ELEPHANT CATCHERS
Key Lessons in Breakthrough Growth
(Revised and Expanded)
Subroto Bagchi

'A must-read for anyone in business.' – *Deccan Herald*

Engaging, wise and thoroughly accessible, *The Elephant Catchers* leads you to evaluate:

- Is your organization's infrastructure designed to evolve and ultimately mimic the simultaneity of a living organism?
- Are you constantly nurturing and renewing your brand identity or letting it stagnate and decay?
- Does your sales force have as many hunters as it has farmers? Or is it dominated by a grizzly who just waits for the salmon to land in its mouth?
- In a fiercely competitive environment, are you really stepping 'out of the box' and learning from unusual sources?

'Practical advice on real issues... Bagchi uses his years of on-the-ground learning and experience to explore [...] what organizations and their people need to do to climb to the next level and beyond.'

– *The Hindu*

'Bagchi's credit lies in his efforts to humanize business... [H]e has always managed to take note of the human at the core...a rare trait in businessmen anywhere.'

– *Business India*

HACHETTE INDIA

Bestselling Business Books

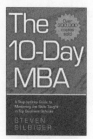

THE 10-DAY MBA

THE 80/20 MANAGER

GIVE AND TAKE

COLD STEEL

START-UP SUTRA

FISH

STEVE JOBS

CHANGE ANYTHING

18 MINUTES

**DON'T SWEAT
THE SMALL STUFF**

HACHETTE INDIA

Bestselling Non-fiction Books

BIG DATA

NOW FOR THEN

THE NEW DIGITAL AGE

THE TIPPING POINT

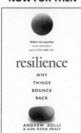

RESILIENCE

ADAPT

THE UNDERCOVER ECONOMIST

THE ART OF THINKING CLEARLY

THE ART OF CHOOSING

JACK, STRAIGHT FROM THE GUT